grow your
personal capital

JUST HOW COULD

GOOD
YOU BE?

grow your
personal capital

what you know, who you know
and how you use it

Hilarie Owen

www.yourmomentum.com
the stuff that drives you

BASIC
BOOKS
A Member of the
Perseus Books Group

What is momentum?

Momentum is a completely new publishing philosophy, in print and online, dedicated to giving you more of the information, inspiration and drive to enhance who you are, what you do, and how you do it.

Fusing the changing forces of work, life and technology, momentum will give you the bright stuff for a brighter future and set you on the way to being all you can be.

Who needs momentum?

Momentum is for people who want to make things happen in their career and their life, who want to work at something they enjoy and that's worthy of their talent and their time.

Momentum people have values and principles, and question who they are, what they do, and who for. Wherever they work, they want to feel proud of what they do. And they are hungry for information, stimulation, ideas and answers ...

Momentum online

Visit *www.yourmomentum.com* to be part of the talent community. Here you'll find a full listing of current and future books, an archive of articles by momentum authors, sample chapters and self-assessment tools. While you're there, post your worklife questions to our momentum coaches and sign up to receive free newsletters with even more stuff to drive you.

If you need more time for your life, try one of these titles, all published under the momentum label.

change activist
make big things happen fast
Carmel McConnell

lead yourself
be where others will follow
Mick Cope

happy mondays
putting the pleasure back into work
Richard Reeves

the big difference
life works when you choose it
Nicola Phillips

snap, crackle or stop
change your career and create your own destiny
Barbara Quinn

float you
how to capitalize on your talent
Carmel McConnell & Mick Cope

innervation
redesign yourself for a smarter future
Guy Browning

coach yourself
make real change in your life
Tony Grant & Jane Greene

Copyright © 2001 by Pearson Education Limited

This edition of *Grow Your Personal Capital: what you know, who you know and how to use it* First Edition is published by arrangement with Pearson Education Limited.

Library of Congress Control Number: 2002116177
ISBN 0-7382-0655-5

Basci Books is a member of the Perseus Books Group.

Find us on the World Wide Web at http://www.basicbooks.com.

Books published by Basic Books are available at special discounts for bulk purchases in the U.S. by corporations, institutions, and other organizations. For more information, please contact the Special Markets Department at the Perseus Books Group, 11 Cambridge Center, Cambridge, MA 02142, or call (800) 255-1514 or (617) 252-5298, or e-mail special.markets@perseusbooks.com.

Concept design by Heat
Production design by Claire Brodmann Book Designs, Lichfield, Staffs

First printing, February 2003

acknowledgements...

I'd like to thank the people who contributed to this book, in particular the individuals who told their stories with honesty and courage to enable you, the reader, to realize that needing to find something 'more' in our work is not unusual.

Many writers have contributed to this with their ideas, theories and views which have given a richness in understanding our human capital.

My thanks also extend to my publishers for their patience and encouragement. In particular I would like to thank Rachael Stock who developed the Momentum series. Her creativity, knowledge and inner wisdom are an example to those wanting to express their own.

I dedicate this book to my colleagues at the Institute of Leadership, in particular to Nigel, Dilys and Brian, whose ideas and hard work have made it possible to offer a network for people who want to become the best they can.

opening

part one
becoming all you can be

part two
knowledge capital

part three
social capital

part four
emotional capital

opening

grow your personal capital

momentum

part five
to be the best you can be

preface

'In the pulse-beat is the life and the longing, all embraced in the great circle of belonging, reaching everywhere, leaving nothing and no one out.'

John O'Donohue

There is a hunger in organizations today. The hunger is driving individuals to find sustenance elsewhere. The hunger is for purpose, meaning and belonging. People want to do more than go to work and do a job. We spend more of our time each day at work than with those we love. Therefore work has to have meaning, it has to involve something larger than ourselves so that we feel we are engaged in something worthwhile. To do this, people desire to express *all* of themselves at work.

When the hunger is not satisfied, people leave, and many of them do not replace the organization with a similar one. This phenomenon I call the 'silent revolution'. More and more of us are looking to express all of ourselves, not part of ourselves. People want to find out who they are when they become the best they can be. They deeply want to express their creativity, vitality, courage and intelligence at work. What prevents this?

There are two barriers. The first is rigid management processes, but the second is far greater – outdated thinking in the heads of many, including our peers and bosses. Today more and more people are searching for a means to be the best they can be, to use all their human capital in the expression of their work. For a decade I have been listening to their stories and needs. I have watched them change their work and develop their human capital to become the best.

grow your personal capital

momentum

Grow Your Personal Capital is for the millions of others who also have this yearning. The book is specifically for anybody who wants to find out who they are and who they can be. (It is *not* a book for HR specialists who want to turn it into a program unless they themselves first develop their human capital and express it in their work. HR specialists must also become the best and develop their full human capital. They too have a journey that is further than study and developing plans.)

Each one of us has this yearning and organizations need to wake up to the need before starvation drives all the best people to search for sustenance elsewhere.

Grow Your Personal Capital should be thought provoking and requires the reader to participate in their unfolding discovery of who they can become. Yet a book is only a book and each individual will see the words differently. In the final analysis only you can decide whether to develop your full humanness.

part one
becoming all you can be

grow your personal capital

momentum

introduction

How many times have you thought, 'I'm sure I am capable of more than I'm using in my present role'? Or wondered, 'just how good could I be if there was purpose and meaning to my work?'.

What is the full expression of your potential? How much more fulfilment could you gain from your work? You are not alone in thinking these thoughts or striving for these goals. In fact, you are one of a growing number of people who are asking the same questions and changing their lives to become all they can be.

A changing picture over time

Two generations ago people went to work on a Monday to do their jobs in factories, shops or offices. They rarely questioned their bosses because they believed the boss should know more than them. These workers did as they were told, for which they received a pay packet at the end of the week.

One generation ago, when the post-war babies went to work, they dared to question the established order in all walks of life. The 1960s saw the young rebelling, only to eventually settle into professions and jobs as they recognized that families need income. What is striking about that generation is that it saw a management class that had been emerging since the 1950s become larger in number as more people were educated to graduate level. For these people the weekly pay packet became a monthly salary and if they were lucky they also had a company car and other financial incentives.

During the 1980s ambition and enterprise were encouraged and rewarded. Women were entering the job market in larger numbers and competing in what had been male domains, including management. A young generation of men and women were growing up believing they could achieve whatever they desired.

Career ladders and job security disappeared

The long recession of the 1990s was a shock to many people. Large-scale downsizing was the popular organizational thinking and shareholder value became a strong driving force. Career ladders and job security disappeared and responsibility was placed with the individual. Today a new generation of workers ranging from 20 to 40 years old has emerged to think, act and want a different way of working. Many are from divorced parents who worked long hours. These 20- or 30-year-olds want to find harmony in their lives, where work, social and home life is balanced and healthy. But their need is more than a work/life balance – the need includes having meaning and purpose in what they do.

Unlike the 1980s, the goal isn't a substantial salary and Porsche but rather work where they contribute to something worthwhile that is appreciated and have time with their friends and family. These people are well educated and recognize that continuous learning and development will enable them to be 'attractive' to any employer. They now realize that security comes from within rather than from a job for life. These people tend to work in offices, but many work from offices at home using technology to connect with others. They also realize that no individual knows everything – especially the boss. However, they acknowledge that information and knowledge are important.

What has evolved in the workplace are 'intelligent workers', often called knowledge workers. Information technology and improved education for more people has played a part in this development. However, intelligent workers are more than individuals who can use a computer or have a certain standard of education – they have a different attitude, expectations and worldview compared to workers previously. Fundamental to this different attitude is the desire to develop as full human beings through their work rather than just do a job, feel secure or earn a certain salary.

Neil's story

Neil has left one global corporate in the financial services for a similar role in a global company in telecommunications. What drove him to this change was the need to develop his human capital.

In my previous job I had opportunities to do new things and was involved to some extent with the organizational development of the company. It was great to work with 'high potentials' and develop a programme for them. However, the company was very selective in what they would spend money on for development. People across the company were not considered – just those who they felt could influence the bottom line.

The most frustrating was the procrastination that was part of the management culture, and lack of funding and support for broader development of all personnel. The relationship with my boss lacked trust and that made it difficult for me to do anything other than what we had done before. Finally, change at the most senior level led to radical changes in vision, direction and commitment to development that was negative.

Now in my new position I have autonomy to map out part of the destiny of the organization within my role. At the same time there is a strong dependency culture where mutual support is everywhere. There is funding to develop programmes; there is a clear vision; there is belief in what we are trying to do; my interest in work has been revitalized through a different industry sector that is growing and has an energy missing in financial services where government regulation has had to be implemented. I have freedom to have creative input into my work; there are new people joining all the time who have a lot to learn; there are opportunities to travel and work cross culturally, with the opportunity to develop the European region.

The learning and development of myself is fundamental to all this. As well as learning a new role and organization I have to build a learning framework that meets the needs of the business that will require developing new frameworks. I also have to learn how to put together a strategy that will work across cultures in Europe where language, culture and diversity come into play, whether it's Germany, Poland or the UK. Finally, I have to learn how to operate as part of a multiple shared leadership where I'm accountable in the UK and US with different attitudes and priorities.

But I am much happier because I feel valued for who I am and what I can contribute. My work now gives me an opportunity to learn, whereas I felt I was being closed down in my last position. Now everything is opening up – I can raise my eyes and look the future in the face rather than hang my head in despair and lack of purpose. I won't ever accept that again. Today I'm working with meaning and purpose, where I can make a difference, and the work pushes all my buttons. There is a hunger for development in the company from others who also want to be the best they can and have meaning to their work. I can help make this happen. That has to be worth more than any salary. I can express my values of trust, fairness, equity of contribution and reward. I can influence change and use all of me instead of only a part.

Neil's biggest problem in his previous role was his 'boss'. So often the biggest block to developing human capital to the full is management control, and in fact research has shown that the most common reason for individuals leaving an organization is their boss. Why do these 'bosses' never change? The two main reasons are control (and with it power) and ego. What is interesting is that the main reason why individuals stay is again their boss, only this time they receive trust, opportunities for growth, open communication and a feeling of being valued.

A 38-year-old colleague of mine has worked for one organization since leaving school. He was successful and happy, leading around 200 people, and the company was more than pleased with his results. A few months ago the company was bought by another in the same market and my colleague found himself with a new boss. This new boss obviously felt 'threatened' and has never encouraged my colleague or acknowledged the hard work the team have put in. Instead new constraints and rules have been put in place, with the result that the only option left to my colleague is to leave.

Sometimes developing your personal capital requires taking courageous steps

Sometimes developing your personal capital requires taking courageous steps, such as leaving the large corporate and trying something new – working for yourself perhaps. The next story shows what can be achieved when an individual accepts the transformation which occurs when developing your human capital.

Nick's story

Nick worked for a well-known global corporate in the food industry. As purchasing manager he had quite a bit of autonomy and development, but it wasn't enough.

Working for this global company was very unrewarding because I could do the job standing on my head and I wasn't driven to climb corporate ladders for the sake of it. I came to a crossroads. At the time there were lots of promotions going on and talk about what people were doing, but I felt apart from it. My appraisals were good and I was pleased for the people who were being made offers, but I felt I was different from my peers. They were always thinking, 'what is my next move?' and looking for promotion. That wasn't what interested me. I didn't fit in with the culture and philosophy of doing business their way where people were just a resource to be used.

I come from a place that sees that we all have something to contribute and give, and that we should help each other rather than focus on self. I like to look for the best in people and believe that we should take responsibility for ourselves and who we can be.

Today my work is providing career outplacement, coaching and counseling on a personal level. The difference is I have no thoughts about what I *should* be doing or what people expect from me. I have purpose and fulfilment. It is very satisfying seeing people realize their potential – to see them move from shock and despondency to achieving what they really want. Although money wasn't a driver I'm earning more than ever and am still surprised by how lucrative my work is. Working for myself means my work fits around me, and my life and the people I meet every week are really interesting.

Most of all there's a framework and purpose now in my work where before I was reacting and living in a situation that wasn't stimulating or comfortable. I will continue working this way for ever. I've gone out and done it and because it works I have no fear or concerns about the future. I'm learning every day and I have meaning and purpose and a reason to get up in the morning.

Before, I was learning skills rather than growing personally. Now I'm learning every day about myself and other people. My understanding of other people's patterns and perspectives is growing and I shall continue with studying to become the best at what I do.

Of course, sometimes transformation from a dreary, frustrating role to a dynamic, challenging one can happen within the same organization.

Debbie's story

Our next story takes us back to financial services where another global company has been the making of an individual.

My role has always been to oversee change and deal with people problems. I always wanted the work to make a valuable contribution and improve the company. However, without position in a hierarchy you end up frustrated. I've always believed that what makes an organization more effective is people. But in this group such a belief is anti-culture.

Time has been my ally as I've been fortunate to work for individuals who have let me plug away and do what I want, which has led to significant results that cannot be hidden. This means the right people have seen sufficient results to know there's something in the work I do even though it's against what managers do. The outcome is they have now put me with people who they know add value to the company but don't 'fit'. Compliance is strong. If a person doesn't fit they are not liked – if they are not liked they are not respected. I have to sort this out. My role is troubleshooter, with a large people aspect to it. It's hard because there is a strong 'boys' club'.

Today I report directly to the chief executive and even here he will say the right words but his actions are still lodged in the 'boys' club' culture. The behaviour is often appalling. However, because I have a reputation and I work closely with the chief, if I ring one of the boys' club they jump. I have never had my phone calls returned so fast. The view is the 'maverick' now has protection and is feared by certain individuals. So I have more authority and responsibility to do what I want and treat people as people, not as a resource, although I'm alone in this.

In my role today I have much more personal growth rather than training and am being stretched doing things I've never done before. An example is dealing with the human side of a recent merger and acquisition. This has made me tougher and I will challenge people more. I love it because I can make a difference. This role will develop all of me, but I'm not committed to the company. I'm getting to the end of my tether with some people. I will do this for a year and then decide what to do next.

These stories demonstrate that intelligent workers want purpose, meaning and values in their work. They also show the importance of learning and personal growth for these people so that they can develop to be the best they can be.

The breaking down of old boundaries of thinking is not just structural but involves employees asking, 'who am I as a person?'. People want to feel a sense of belonging and be part of something larger than themselves.

Intelligent workers are emerging everywhere – in large corporate organizations, small businesses, schools, hospitals, the armed forces. There is a transformation under way in the workplace, and it's not an initiative or reaction to outside forces. What is occurring is a transformation being driven by individuals *inside* organizations. We can call it the desire to 'grow your human capital'. What this means is learning to make the fullest use of your potential and the extraordinary power you have inside you in all aspects of your life. Developing your human capital is about becoming the best you can be. It involves learning, reflection, growing and finding meaning and purpose in your work.

We can call it the desire to 'grow your human capital'

Many employers, managers and HR specialists see only the tip of the iceberg in employees while underneath most of the potential and capability remain hidden. To fully develop and make the whole human being visible there is a need to look both deep inside people and out into the world to better understand it.

Grow Your Personal Capital is a practical, self-learning guide to achieving the fulfilment of your potential as a human being. Growing is more than physical. As children we grow taller and stronger; our knowledge and awareness grow as well as our understanding of the environment and world we live in. Yet inside every child there is also creativity, self-worth, feelings, self-awareness, consciousness, beliefs and energy. Watch small children play and you will see that growth and development are far more than physical.

Likewise, as adults we see growth as developing more skills, learning a new language, developing relationships and improving what we do. Inside each adult is still creativity, self-worth, beliefs, self-awareness, consciousness and energy – but are we growing these through our work? Growing means nurturing and developing you – all of you. It means recognizing that intelligent workers are everywhere in organizations, looking to fulfill their potential, learn and have purpose in the work they do.

The challenge

Peter Senge wrote about developing individuals in *The Fifth Discipline* (Currency/Doubleday, 1990). Here he explains the challenge:

'(It) goes beyond competence and skills, although it is grounded in competence and skills. It goes beyond spiritual unfolding or opening, although it requires spiritual growth. It means approaching one's life as a creative work, living life from a creative as opposed to reactive viewpoint.'

All too often we spend our time at work reacting to everything around us. It is so easy to get distracted and forget what we really want to do. One of the hardest challenges today is to 'stay in the moment' and not be distracted by phone calls, too many meetings and other people making demands. It is exhausting and unproductive.

It's no wonder that personal growth and development – with the aim of being a more effective and fulfilled person – is the goal of more and more of us today. This need goes beyond the workplace and includes social and family life. But what this book also tackles is the nebulous question, 'what is it we are trying to become?'.

This process of 'becoming' and growing is part of the wider evolutionary story of life; it is the story of becoming true human 'beings'. It shows how connected we are to all life in the universe as each living thing grows to take its place on the planet. As such, just as we consciously create the 'best' conditions for plants to grow, we also need to identify the best conditions for people to grow and one of these areas is work.

There is a negative characteristic to growth

However, as human beings with free will we need to recognize how individuals make 'growth decisions'. There is a negative characteristic to growth that Peter Senge observed. It would seem that growth begins, builds momentum and then either forms a plateau or stops. For example, an organization may decide to implement quality circles or business process re-engineering (BPR). There is initial movement but after a while most of the work stops as it becomes a threat to individuals. A simpler example is when someone begins a diet or decides to give up smoking as a way of improving their health. At first they try really hard and notice some quick loss of weight or get through a few days without a cigarette. Then the pressure to revert is so great they weaken and go back to their old behaviors.

In personal growth I've seen graduates who are keen and hungry to develop, but when they get to their early forties they reach a plateau and stop growing. This problem can be seen in many board directors who stopped developing years before. What is interesting is that I have found some chief executives differ from their board – they actively proceed to grow, and not just in business skills but in emotional intelligence, self-awareness and spiritually. Therefore growing your human capital is for everyone – no matter what your role or position.

For those who have stopped growing (and this can happen in a person's twenties or thirties) life is full of external 'things' – a job title, car, income. The ego is being fed and this is quite addictive. These people continue to seek a bigger salary, a bigger car, a bigger bonus. What is actually happening is that they are avoiding looking inside themselves, which requires real courage. Often a 'life crisis' forces them to take this inner journey that leads to growth and happiness.

At the beginning of a new century, with new technology and new challenges for our world, it has never been more important for organizations to embrace people who want to grow. For it will be these people who will innovate, strive to serve customers, and provide creativity, passion and leadership in a fast-changing world.

Getting the most from this book

Can you really learn how to become the best you can be from a book? If you read this book with an open mind and believe that there is something to learn from every experience every day, then you are already on your way. To enhance this, I suggest there is a further way to learn from reading this book. If you participate in the process and become actively involved while reading, you will get more out of it. I suggest that you take an exercise book and pen and use these for the tasks and exercises you will find in each chapter that will enhance the learning process.

We all have goals concerning our personal life and work

I don't know why, but the process of writing has a positive effect. We all have goals concerning our personal life and work. When we write them down, for some reason they are more likely to happen. In the same way, if you can participate in the learning from this book through writing you will find it shapes your thinking into a perspective and improves the understanding of yourself and the world we all live in. And in doing so you create a record of your thinking at this moment in time that you can use as a base and can revisit to see change and evaluate the learning process.

We live and work in a transforming world. Nature shows us that during such times the need for learning has to be equal to or greater than the change itself. Therefore *Grow Your Personal Capital* is a learning journey to become the best you can be in a world that will be different tomorrow from today.

Psychologist Carl Rogers described those people who would be able to live and work in a transforming world, identifying certain traits they would tend to have. Here's a check list and see how many of those traits you carry. Answer the questions with a 'yes' or 'no'.

List of characteristics and questions relating to them

Read the characteristic and answer yes or no to each question.

1. Openness.

Are you open to new experiences?

Do new ways of seeing the world excite you?

Can you quickly grasp new ideas and concepts?

2. Desire for authenticity.

Are you a good communicator?

Do you love telling stories and painting pictures to explain things?

Do you hate hypocrisy and deceit?

3. Scepticism with science and technology.

Do you distrust the science we use to conquer nature?

Do you hate science that tries to control people?

Do you support science and technology that enhances people's lives without control?

4. Desire for wholeness.

Do you see human beings as being body, mind, spirit and emotion?

Do you disagree with separating intellect and feelings?

Do you see all life as integrated?

5. **The wish for intimacy.**

   Do you seek shared purpose and support at work?

   Do you enjoy closeness in relationships at work?

   Do you prefer to have verbal rather than non-verbal communication?

6. **Process people.**

   Is change the one certainty in life?

   Are you comfortable with risk taking?

   Do you work at changing yourself for the better?

7. **Caring.**

   Are you eager to help others?

   Is your caring non-moralistic and non-judgmental?

   Are you suspicious of the 'professional' helper?

8. **Attitude towards nature.**

   Do you feel close to nature?

   Do you take an active role in the ecology of the world?

   Do you care for nature in your actions and decisions?

9. **Anti-institutional.**

   Do you have difficulties with inflexible, bureaucratic institutions?

   Do you believe organizations are for people rather than the opposite?

   Do you have difficulty working in a highly structured organization?

10. **The authority within.**

    Do you trust your experience and intuition?

    Do you make your own moral judgements even if it means breaking the law?

    Do you distrust external authorities?

11. The unimportance of material things.

Are your main goals other than money and material status symbols?

Can you live with affluence without it being necessary to your happiness?

Do you look for rewards that are non-material?

12. A yearning for the spiritual.

Do you yearn for meaning and purpose in your life?

Is inner peace a goal for you?

Have you ever experienced a feeling of being in harmony with the universe?

The more times you have answered 'yes', the more likely you are to be aware and part of the transformation taking place in the workplace. You are one of many who want to develop their human capital with the aim of being 'all you can be'. This is not a selfish pursuit for it stems from a belief that all humans are worthy. So how can you develop your personal capital? What *is* your personal capital? What are the changes in thinking required to achieve this goal? The next chapter will try to answer these questions. However, before we move on, another story.

So how can you develop your personal capital?

There was a little girl in the hospital suffering from a rare and serious disease. Her only chance of recovery seemed to be a blood transfusion from her five-year-old brother who had miraculously survived the same disease and developed the antibodies needed to combat the illness.

The doctors explained the situation to the boy and asked him if he would be willing to give his blood to his sister. He hesitated for only a moment before saying, 'yes, I'll do it if it will save her'.

During the transfusion the little boy lay in a bed next to his sister and smiled when he saw the color returning to her cheeks. Then his face grew pale and his smile faded. He looked up at the doctor and asked with a trembling voice, 'will I start to die right away?'.

The little boy had misunderstood the doctor and thought he was giving all his blood to his sister in order to save her.

Understanding and *attitude* are very important, as this story shows, and nonetheless so when exploring human capital. This book will try to provide the information you need to understand. However, it will be your attitude that will decide how much you use this understanding to develop your human capital. No process of human development is easy, but attitude can make the difference between an average response and a life-changing transformation. Viktor Frankl wrote about his life doing hard labour in Nazi concentration camps (*Man's Search for Meaning*, Simon & Schuster, 1984):

'Everything can be taken away from a man but one thing, the last of the human freedoms – to choose one's attitude in any given set of circumstances, to choose one's way ...'

Viktor Frankl and his family were arrested by the Nazis during the second world war and he spent three years in Auschwitz. Every member of his family, including his parents, his siblings and his pregnant wife, was killed. Despite horrific, abusive and degrading conditions, Viktor survived.

After his liberation by Allied troops he wrote about the need for meaning in our lives for he had discovered that even under inhuman conditions, people can live with purpose and meaning. Prisoners at Auschwitz saw a world that didn't value human life or dignity, a world that took away their will and made them worthless objects to be exterminated, a world where their values were crushed and where a meaningful life seemed impossible. Viktor Frankl found that if people did not fight for their self-respect and human spirit, they lost their connection with the feeling of being a person, an individual with inner freedom, a mind and values. This individual would become so deeply depressed they would become incapable of action, merely wandering around until they died.

Viktor Frankl clung to the meaning that he must help his fellow prisoners and he tried to find ways for them to look forward to the future. Incentives ranged from anticipating seeing a loved one waiting for their return, to completing unfinished work or returning to a special talent.

Each of us searches for meaning, to make a unique contribution to the world and to live a life that has purpose, using all we are capable of. Each one of us seeks to be all we can be. *Grow Your Personal Capital* is for all those who seek to be the best in every aspect of their lives.

chapter one
from parts to whole

What is human capital?

There is no doubt that we are seeing a rise in intelligent workers who want to develop their human capital, but does developing human capital mean increasing people's knowledge? Sumantra Ghoshal from the London Business School said: 'Often we make the mistake of thinking of human capital as just knowledge. A second important aspect is social capital – networks and relationships. The third dimension is emotional – the ability and willingness to act' (*The Individualized Corporation* – with Christopher Bartlett – Harper Business, 1997). Thus showing that human capital is much more than the knowledge in people's heads.

Human capital is the full expression of an individual at their best

In fact, human capital is the full expression of an individual at their best. It involves the 'whole' human being – knowledge, social, emotional, intuitive and physical. Bringing this together as a synthesis is the aim of this book. You will find that chapters relate to other chapters. This is because we are trying to explain all aspects of your human capital and each will link to others, so each chapter is not a separate 'part' but connected to the rest. This approach is central to the whole book.

In our world today we have based science, medicine, organizations and management on a philosophy of breaking things up into parts or pieces. If I have a pain in my back I see a back specialist who will focus on my back. However, the pain may originate somewhere else but be more painful in a part of my back. Dealing with my back may take away some pain for a while but over time the pain will return because the real cause has not been identified.

We break organizations into parts in the form of departments or 'silos'. If one is not performing as well as the others we try to sort out the department, but again the real cause of the problem may come from another part of the organization. The focus in organizations is on making each piece or part successful in the belief that this will add up to the whole. We neglect the relationships between the parts and this is why most change initiatives fail or become diluted.

There is growing recognition that the relationships among the parts, and between the whole and the part, are what matters. When looking at human capital we have to look at the whole person and the relationships between the parts that make up that individual.

Seeing the whole

For a while now we have heard people in organizations say that the most important resource is people, but their actions and behaviour show the contrary. Today intelligent workers are using their feet to respond to this. Managers and directors need to change their mindset from seeing people as parts to seeing them as whole human beings. It is no longer sufficient for us to think in terms of parts or building blocks; we have to look at the whole and relationships within the whole in organizations and individuals. This type of thinking is called 'systems thinking' or general systems theory.

One of the well-known biologists who espoused systems thinking was Ludwig von Bertalanffy, who said: 'General systems theory is a general science of "wholeness" ...' (*General Systems Theory*, Braziller, 1968).

Author Marilyn Ferguson explained this approach when she wrote that a systems view:

'... sees all of nature – including human behaviour – as interconnected. According to General Systems Theory, nothing can be understood in isolation but must be seen as part of a system ... In relationship there is novelty, creativity, richer complexity. Whether we are talking about chemical reactions or human societies, molecules or international treaties, there are qualities that cannot be predicted by looking at the components.'

(*The Aquarian Conspiracy*, Granada, 1982)

Therefore by just focusing on knowledge intelligence or just focusing on emotional intelligence we miss the relationships between these and the whole of a human being. Systems thinking is contextual – instead of taking things apart to understand them, systems thinking requires putting them into the context of a larger whole.

Fritjof Capra, director of the Center for Ecoliteracy, in Berkeley, California, wrote:

'The systems view looks at the world in terms of relationships and integration. Systems are integrated wholes whose properties cannot be reduced to those of smaller units. Instead of concentrating on basic building blocks or basic substances, the systems approach emphasizes basic principles of organization.'

(*The Web of Life*, HarperCollins, 1996)

Synergy – the whole is more than the sum of the parts – is very important to the shift from parts to whole. This shift is also one from seeing objects to seeing relationships. In the past (and for many still today) we have seen organizations and people as objects or things. This worldview is known as the 'mechanistic' view that sees organizations as machines. Within these machines are people who are perceived as cogs or resources. Management is required to create order and assume the worst of people. This means that management's role is one of control, putting people into boxes and treating them as objects.

Network of relationships

The systems worldview is to see organizations as places full of human beings who are in relationships with everyone else, including suppliers and customers. In other words there are networks of relationships throughout. Within these relationships are ideas, creativity, talent and knowledge – all that is required to make an organization successful. Yet few organizations know how to release this talent. They haven't realized that what is required is developing the whole person and unblocking the rigid processes of control. When this happens, the relationships between people become dynamic and synergistic.

The relationships between people become dynamic and synergistic

It is the dynamics of the relationships that make the whole paramount in developing human capital. Take a simple example. Play a musical note. What does it mean? Very little on its own. Play a sheet of music and what you experience is the relationship of the notes with each other.

We can take this further. Having heard the sheet of music there are at least two ways of understanding it. We can ask, what is the piece called? How is it similar or different to other pieces? This one-dimensional understanding is often found in our education system. A deeper understanding comes from asking, what does the piece mean? How does it relate to others? How does it fit into the symphony it came from?

Think back to your school days and remember the different subjects you studied, or if you have taken an MBA think of the subjects you covered. Did you ever find that some of the learning in geography related to history? Or how marketing related to economics? Yet when you asked this question you were immediately told the other subject was separate and all you had to do was learn what was being taught for your exams. This is why education as it is has a limiting outcome for even the most clever of academics if this 'separate parts' approach is endorsed. The same is true when trying to understand human potential at work.

Taking the whole human being and seeing the potential hasn't just been the approach of systems thinking. At the beginning of the 20th century psychologist Carl Jung rebelled against the rigid, often 'dark' thinking of Freud and developed a view of the whole human being. Jung believed that the personality we acquire through our upbringing and social conditioning is only part of what makes us what and who we are. Within us is a deeper, wiser being that he called the 'eternal Self' that is unique to each of us and is the centre of our consciousness. He believed that when all aspects of our complex personality or being are integrated, we can become truly individual, unique and all we are capable of being.

There is no doubt that we can shape ourselves into the person we want to be and construct a fulfilling life. Jung recognized that the process is difficult but deep in our unconsciousness is a 'map' with signposts that will help us take the inner journey of our own evolution. What prevents us, according to Jung, are not symptoms that are external or even internal, but the whole person. Therefore Jung believed focusing on the whole person was the right way to develop what we call here 'human capital'. So let's begin the process of exploring your whole being.

Exercise

Write your full name at the top of a blank page. Then on the page brainstorm as many words as you can to describe the named person.

This is your first attempt to see your whole self and it will be interesting to return to this page at the end and see how much more you can add when you have finished reading the book and learned about all that makes you the person you are.

A simple holistic model for learning and transforming ourselves to be all we can be comes from Robert Dilts an NLP practitioner and academic (see Figure 1.1). He argues that learning takes place at different levels but when developed together the effect is long lasting. These levels are:

◆ **Environment** – this is what you react to and includes your surroundings, the people you meet and those you work with. Your environment began to influence you from the moment you were born. Over time you have built a picture of the larger environment that we call the universe. How do you react to everything in your world? Developing your human capital will help you discover this.

◆ **Behavior** – these are the actions you carry out regardless of capabilities. Behavior follows patterns that we tend to repeat until the beliefs much deeper change. Our behavior will result in how well we get along with colleagues and interact in the world. Very often training looks at changing behavior, but can you now see that to really change an individual has to learn at a much deeper level?

◆ **Capability** – this is your general skills and strategies that you use in your daily life. It is your knowledge capital and is more easily developed as we are still quite near to the surface of who we are. However, even here, some individuals are not 'aware' of their full capabilities. Developing your whole human capital means knowing and using these skills.

◆ **Beliefs** – here are the ideas which you hold as true and which affect your daily life. These beliefs give you permission to do things but they also limit what you believe you can do. Beliefs are powerful and in developing our whole selves and changing parts of ourselves knowing these beliefs will be fundamental. How often have you heard someone say they believe in something but

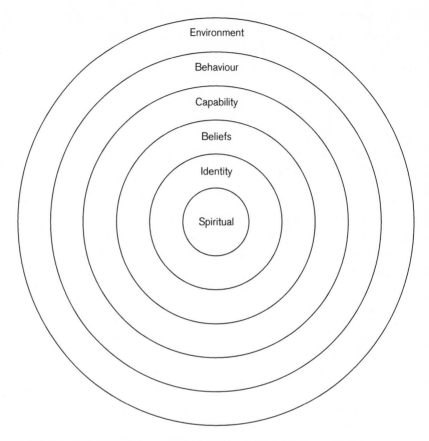

Figure 1.1 A simple holistic model for learning and transforming ourselves
Based on Robert Dilts' work

their actions show otherwise? This is because they have not changed their deeply held beliefs. This layer is getting deeper.

◆ **Identity** – this is your basic sense of self along with your core values and mission. Our sense of self influences how we perceive everyone else and how we respond to others. Our core values are so important that if we try to live outside them we are never happy. Therefore developing our human capital will enable us to identify these core values.

◆ **Spiritual** – this is your deepest level and here we ask questions such as 'why are we here?' and 'what is our purpose?'. This is the level of who you are. The problem is that most people don't know who they are or who they are capable of being. In developing our human capital, our whole being, we need to work at this deepest level.

The holistic model works on this basis: that the deeper or more to the center each of these levels is, the more they will impact on and relate to the other levels. Therefore change at the spiritual level will affect all the levels. While change in environment is unlikely to change your beliefs, change in your beliefs will change how you behave. In fact, identity and beliefs will have a profound impact on your 'potential'.

The deepest change will come from the center – the spiritual level

The deepest change will come from the center – the spiritual level. Spirit here does not have an organized religious meaning but rather a deep self-knowing of who and what you are and your place in the universe. The wonder of this level of learning is not only the love and inner peace you find but a wisdom that is greater than any knowledge you will acquire from books or study. Jung saw this learning as a journey to meet Self and the Divine. To leave this out would mean leaving out the center of the whole human being and we would not have a full picture of human capital.

As you follow the journey of discovery through this book you will delve deep within yourself until you find the truth that is your identity. It will be a journey of self-exploration and discovery to find your authentic self that is your whole human capital.

Impact of gender today

Many men today are no longer the sole breadwinner but have changed their role to one of an equal partner and parent, taking time to be with their children and to participate in their development.

Men are becoming whole as they develop their caring side. Women, on the other hand, are showing their whole beings by achieving in education and in their careers. However, there is a problem for some people who work in a male-dominated environment such as financial services, the armed forces or the police force, where sometimes neither men nor women are allowed to show their caring side. For women this can be particularly difficult. Susan Wittig Albert describes this in her book *Work of Her Own* (G.P. Putnam's Sons, 1992):

'We easily recognize a woman at the pinnacle of her career. She is a self-realized, self-determined, stand-alone person. She has an autonomous, independent identity, the major components of which include her work, her title, and the status and prestige that come with the titles – all conferred by the work institution to which she belongs. She has successfully climbed the masculine staircase of adult growth and development ... As she moves up the work world, the successful woman is required to repudiate most of what makes her a woman: her feminine viewpoint, her feminine values of nurturing and caring. In order to succeed she develops a strongly male-oriented bias and a tendency to uphold and defend the masculine culture of ideas and ideals ...'

Some women recognize this loss of part of themselves and they leave their organization to do something totally different as a way of 'redefining themselves'. What they are in fact doing is trying to develop their whole being. This need to develop our whole being is universal. Human beings are transforming. We are following a path we are meant to follow towards the fulfilment of our human potential. To achieve this, we must take on board whole systems thinking rather than seeing only parts. The question remains, what is the end goal? What is our potential?

For psychologist Abraham Maslow, best known for his hierarchy of needs model, the goal was 'peak experience', which was the ultimate in self-actualization. He believed that peak experience was what you feel and 'know' when you achieve authentic transcendence as a human being.

What is becoming clear, and is certainly my belief, is that this peak experience and achieving authentic transcendence takes place internally, as an inner journey. The external world and knowledge give people opportunities to learn and to use the experience for an inner process. However, ultimately it is the individual who chooses to learn and grow to peak experience. This begs the question: why is it that some people achieve peak experience while most others do not or do it to a much lesser degree? This was a question Maslow could not answer. We will try.

Something I have noticed is that many people look outside in the world for their answers to feel worthy, needed and loved. They may look for status or a big car, or may build a dependency relationship with their children or partner. When these people become aware of looking outside for identity and recognition and try to change, they have to face what is *inside* them and that requires courage and time. However, if they are successful, these people develop an inner wisdom of who they are, what is really important to them and how they can find meaning and purpose through their work.

They have to face what is *inside* them

For this reason I believe we can bring the work of Maslow and Jung together for an even deeper understanding of how to attain peak experience and start to resolve the question of why some and not others. Jung developed his model of extroverts and introverts that may help solve this riddle, for I believe that to reach peak experience there is a need to stop looking outside, which extroverts tend to do, and instead look inside as introverts in a quiet environment.

According to Jung, extroverts respond to the world around them. They love parties and games. Extroverts volunteer as organizers and lend people their cars and clothes. They communicate well and have no difficulty starting up conversations with strangers. Extroverts need an audience and someone to listen to them. They find out what they think by talking their ideas through with others rather than thinking things out in their mind. They make good sales and marketing people, fashion, media and advertising executives. Physical extroverts are attracted to the armed forces, want to become lifeguards and excel as mountain expedition leaders.

Introverts are different in that they have good concentration and so enjoy reading and studying and are often ahead for their age when they start school. Introverts like parties when they know the people invited. A room full of strangers is an ordeal. An introverted friend is a friend for life because they work at maintaining contact. They have the patience to learn complex skills and are happy undergoing solitary training, making field and track events or tennis more appealing than rugby or football. Introverts think deeply, which can lead to original ideas for a novel or scientific research. Long study doesn't put introverts off, so many become lawyers, doctors and engineers.

What Jung's work on this shows us is that we each have a tendency to be more of one of these orientations. However, I believe you can learn to sometimes reach the other orientation. Being an introvert, when I tried speaking in public for the first time I was so terrified that my whole body, including my voice, trembled. My mind went blank and the audience became a blur. Today I speak at conferences worldwide without nerves. I learned, and made myself use every opportunity to practice, to reach this point – it wasn't natural. The tendency inside me is still to be alone and I use this to replenish my energy. Yet I can stand in front of a large audience and actually enjoy touching others with ideas and knowledge.

Therefore I believe an individual can learn to develop some of the abilities of their opposite orientation. If extroverts adapt and find the courage to be alone to reflect, they will find it easier to look inwards. Coming out of our natural state is sometimes painful, but it is part of developing our whole being – our human capital. This is what this book will try to help individuals achieve.

With that thought take five minutes to solve this mystery.

Exercise

Bill and Hillary are lying dead and naked, in a locked room with an open window. In the middle of the room is an overturned chair surrounded by a pool of water and broken glass. Who are Bill and Hillary and how did they die? Write the answer in your exercise book.

We will return to this in a moment when all will be revealed. In the meantime, if you are going to use this book to develop your human capital, we need to conclude this chapter with some information on learning.

Learning to learn

When we think of learning we tend to think of a new skill or a child learning their times tables. In fact, learning is quite complex and does not always follow a straightforward process.

One way we learn is by consciously mastering small pieces of behaviour, then combining them into larger chunks that become habitual and unconscious. This leaves room for new learning following the same process as the conscious mind is quite limiting.

Our unconscious on the other hand is all the life-giving processes of our body, all our experiences, and all that we might notice but do not in any present moment. In our day-to-day lives, most of what we do we do unconsciously.

When we look at the word 'learning' in Chinese symbols it is interesting how another culture perceives it. The first character means to study and has a symbol meaning 'to accumulate knowledge' above a symbol for a child in a doorway. This notion of seeing learning as a doorway is very powerful and goes deeper than the idea of gaining qualifications. The second character means to practise constantly and shows a bird developing the ability to leave the nest. The upper symbol represents flying, which I think also means freedom – the freedom to become. The second symbol stands for youth. For the Chinese, learning is ongoing and centred around self-improvement. But is it the case that learning always begins with consciously mastering a piece of behavior?

Learning is ongoing and centered around self-improvement

Swiss developmental psychologist Jean Piaget watched children develop and identified two types of learning. The first he called 'learning by assimilation' which involves taking information for which the learner already has structures in place to recognize and give meaning to the signal. This learning involves being exposed to facts and assimilating them intellectually. This type of learning is carried out in schools and universities involving teachers.

The second form of learning Piaget called 'learning by accommodation'. This is where learning involves an internal structural change in your beliefs, ideas and attitudes and requires much more than books and teachers. It is an experiential process by which you adapt to a changing world through in-depth processes in which you participate fully – with all your intellect *and* heart, not knowing what the final outcome will be, only that you will be different afterwards.

Learning by accommodation comes through the inter-relationship with the environment that enables you to grow, survive and develop your full potential. Arie de Geus sums this up brilliantly when he says: 'Our individual behaviour can be explained only by understanding the internal force of our goals and teleological drive, together with the forces coming from the outside environment' (*The Living Company*, Harvard Business School Press, 1997).

This form of learning is what I call 'deep learning' and life-long. So how do we learn to learn so that we can develop our whole human potential – our human capital?

Building on the work of Jean Piaget, John Dewey (American philosopher and educator) and Kurt Lewin (an organizational psychologist), David Kolb, an American professor of management, took their ideas and synthesized their work, expanding it to develop a model for learning (see Figure 1.2). In understanding this model the first step is to realize that it is a continuous process, but let's begin with reflecting.

Reflecting

This is where an individual becomes aware of their own thinking, feelings and behaviour in what they do. This step requires questioning beliefs, thinking, feelings and actions. Remember that these are deep inside you and require time.

Connecting

This is the creative step where new ideas emerge and possibilities are explored.

Deciding

Once explored, you decide your option and method of action.

Doing

You achieve your task using your new frame of mind. On completion you quickly move to reflection, where you ask how the task went.

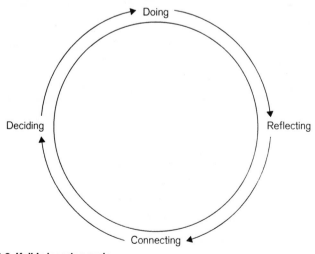

Figure 1.2 Kolb's learning cycle

grow your personal capital

In Japan people would spend much time reflecting

Working with different cultures I found people move around at different times. For example, in Japan people would spend much time reflecting and connecting before deciding and doing. However, when they did reach the doing, it worked well. In the UK and US people tend to be more task oriented and therefore often rush the first two stages and get to doing quickly, only to find it doesn't work and they have to go round again.

David Kolb suggests that most people will have a natural leaning towards one or two stages of the cycle. From this Honey and Mumford (see Appendix) produced their work on learning styles in the UK. To find out yours there is a questionnaire in the Appendix. Understanding your natural style of learning will help you here.

Let's return to Bill and Hillary. The answer is that Bill and Hillary are goldfish which died when their bowl of water was knocked off the stool by a strong gust of wind through the open window.

Did you think they were human? Were you influenced by the association with Bill and Hillary Clinton? Did the word 'naked' lead you to assume they were people? How many times a day do you take limited information and create inaccurate assumptions and scenarios around it? (This exercise came from my friend and colleague Liz Simpson.)

When we look at the whole – the room with the open window, the broken glass, the water and so on – without limiting beliefs or assumptions, we can find the truth. When we look at the whole human being without limiting beliefs and assumptions, we can find the authentic individual who has the potential to achieve anything. This is human capital.

We are now going to start peeling back the layers that make up a whole human being. Think of an onion with layers and in the centre a shining bulbous heart. We will begin with an outside layer that has deeper components as we peel it back.

part two
knowledge capital

chapter two
the knowledge at your fingertips

We will begin peeling back your human capital with an outside layer that you often show to the world – your knowledge. Within this knowledge are deeper and deeper layers.

The knowledge at your fingertips is made up of information stored from childhood. In school you learned your times tables, dates in history, mathematical equations, songs, spelling and so on. From the time you are born the brain is memorizing and storing information and knowledge. Much of it is rarely used and most of the information is subliminal. However, there is a difference between information and knowledge.

Information vs knowledge

We use information for pre-planned responses to anticipated stimuli, whereas knowledge consists of unplanned, innovative responses to surprising stimuli, thus giving knowledge a component of creativity. So knowledge is much more than information – something many organizations haven't grasped yet.

There is growing recognition that knowledge is important to organizations, and that includes people's ideas. One of the reasons for this recognition of knowledge in individuals has been the increase in education, particularly graduate education, since the 1950s. At the same time the past decade has seen a drive for quality transform to a drive for innovation. This innovation needs to at least keep up and renew with changing markets. It is now recognized that innovation in products and services is what makes the difference in a fast changing, greater, more competitive marketplace.

Let's explore knowledge as an essential element of your human capital.

Exercise

In your exercise book work through each of these headings, making notes describing your knowledge for each heading.

Professional area of expertise
Social relationships
Religion
Science
Aesthetics (beauty, art, etc.)
Human beings
Moral issues
History
Children
Literature
Technology

Now draw a clock shape and give each topic a slice according to how much knowledge you have on these topics.

Suddenly you have the first view of your knowledge capital. What else can we learn about knowledge? Knowledge is about connections. It comes from a collection of multiple experiences and perspectives, and learning from books, life and work makes up an individual 'knowledge base'.

In organizations there is a tendency to treat knowledge as collecting and disseminating information when in fact knowledge is about connecting with others and sharing your knowledge bases.

Knowledge is about connecting with others

It is often considered that knowledge is internalized and personal to each individual, making it different to information. However, British philosopher Michael Polanyi identified two types of knowledge in his 1960s' writings: explicit and tacit.

Two types of knowledge

Explicit knowledge can be articulated in formal language and transmitted among individuals. For example, when someone is teaching another person how to use computer graphics, they are using explicit knowledge. *Tacit* knowledge is personal knowledge embedded in individual experience that involves the person's beliefs, values and perspectives.

This challenges the above view that *all* knowledge is internalized. Although Polanyi wrote this in the 1960s, the information technology revolution of the 21st century shows that explicit knowledge can be articulated and passed on to others. In addition, there are two sides to tacit knowledge. As a source of knowledge it is invaluable, but tacit knowledge can also be a problem in that it can be wrong, it's hard to change, and it's difficult to communicate. Remember you are dealing with deep issues here such as beliefs, values and perspectives that are personal and individual.

Technology and telecommunications are useful for dealing with explicit knowledge, but they cannot deal with implicit knowledge. In a world where changing customer needs and innovative products and services are required more and more, you will be required to use your tacit knowledge. Therefore we need to explore this resource you have as part of your human capital.

Tacit knowledge is stored in your mind essentially as a combination of experience, judgement and intuition. It is powerful for you but it is difficult to share; with tacit knowledge you know more than you can tell. So how can you tap it?

Exercise

Allow at *least* an hour — this isn't something you can rush as it is important and it is worth it. First do a brainstorm of all the memorable events in your life, both good and bad. Write down as many as you can. Now take a clean sheet and starting with your earliest memories describe all your experiences. Put in all the people who influenced you and all the learning from the experiences. Keep writing until you are up to today. There is no hurry and it is normal to remember events later and return to add them in.

Are there patterns of repeated experiences? Ask the question: what am I not learning that I should be? Go through each and record whether it was happy or sad. Do you find you learned more from the sad or difficult?

You now have documentation of most of your experiences. The final step is to go through each: what was the experience? What did you learn? What do you know now that you didn't know then? How do you feel about the lessons? What would you do today if the same situation occurred? Would you recognize the experience before going through it again? What advice would you give to others from this experience?

Ask these questions all the way through and you will fill pages of implicit knowledge. It is even more effective to do this with someone you trust and share the learning, although for that you need to put aside two to three hours.

What you achieve is clear understanding of the tacit knowledge you hold that is part of your human capital. This understanding fits with the views of Keith Todd, former chief executive of ICL, who also argues for two types of knowledge. The first needs to be *shared*, while the second needs to be *created*. Todd adds: 'I feel strongly that there is a relationship between sharing knowledge efficiently and giving time back for reflection. Creating knowledge needs time for reflection' (*Financial Times*, 1 October 1997).

Making time to reflect on your experiences is the way to draw out the knowledge that is there. The problem is, as you can now see – it takes time. Nevertheless, the value and benefits of doing this far outweigh this disadvantage.

Remnants of the past

Time is a rare commodity these days, leaving the creative process of knowledge under-utilized. Our history of work organizations has left us remnants such as 'you're not paid to think, you are here to work'. In other words, work is activity, not thinking. This is strongly reflected in work cultures in the UK and US.

Another remnant is 'we pay you for your skills to do what works, not to question my decisions'. This is another message that thinking as an individual is not valued at work and that skill is only what you provide while you're there. Kiichi Mochizuki of the Pacific Institute in New York says: 'When you talk about skill, the word "skill" is wrong: it implies manual dexterity to carve the wood or hit something with a hammer. Now skill is mental rather than manual' (Thomas Stewart, *Intellectual Capital*, Doubleday, 1997).

Employees are encouraged to learn everything

Another misconception is that knowledge is only in the heads of graduates or 'fast track' employees. Yet on the outskirts of San Juan in Puerto Rico a factory for knowledge work has become part of everyone's job. Here blue-collar workers become knowledge workers and the whole organization is constantly learning. Employees change jobs every six months, rotating through the factory's four work areas. This means everyone not only knows how to do all the work but also knows how each area depends on the others on the line. In addition, employees are encouraged to learn everything from machine maintenance to English and business studies. The rewards for this are financial bonuses. Promotion is based on what people know, not seniority. How does this compare to where you work? How do you feel about this? Developing your knowledge capital requires reflection and understanding the beliefs that shape what you consider to be knowledge.

Our beliefs are guiding principles with which we make sense of the world, built from our experiences and from other people. They come from our upbringing, role models, past traumas and repetitive experiences. The power of our beliefs can be illustrated by what is known as the placebo effect. Here patients with serious illnesses improve if they believe they are being given an effective drug when in fact they are being given placebos – inert substances.

Deep beliefs

Beliefs are not only powerful but also deep. Psychologist Chris Argyris found that in organizations individuals say certain things believing them to be true, but when a crisis erupts their real beliefs emerge. For example, directors may say we believe in our people and see them as the best asset, but their actions will prove to be contrary in a crisis, resulting in large redundancies with senior managers given five minutes to clear their desks before being marched off the premises by security. Therefore to explore beliefs requires deep reflection and questioning.

Some of your beliefs are profound, with far-reaching implications; others will be less significant. But together they form your personal philosophy of life that will influence the part of your knowledge capital known as tacit knowledge. This knowledge will be shown to the world through your behaviour and choices that you make every day. You create yourself and your destiny through those choices. So your knowledge capital is an important part of your human capital and much, much more than the storage of information. Also the types of knowledge and how we use knowledge is changing.

Author Thomas Stewart also identifies two forms of knowledge. He says there is the 'semi-permanent body of knowledge' which he identifies as the expertise that develops with a task, a person or an organization. This could be an individual working in a role over time and building an expertise and knowledge base for that role that only the individual owns. Then there are the 'tools that augment the body of knowledge' (*Intellectual Capital*, Doubleday, 1997). This is where facts, expertise, data or information are provided to those who need them *when* they need them. Here a new situation arises and the individual searches out the knowledge, perhaps on the Internet, as they require it to resolve a problem or deal with an unusual request.

Stewart's argument is that in the past the first form of knowledge was prevalent and was often guarded as it was perceived as a form of power, while today the second form of knowledge is required to a greater degree and shows the importance of connections, whether through technology or through relationships.

Do we need management?

Another aspect of knowledge work is that it doesn't happen the way mechanical labour did and it therefore challenges our present views on management. Do we need management? If knowledge and leadership are expressed throughout organizations, why should there be a need for managers? Managers are custodians – they are present to keep order. If individuals express their whole human capital, the focus shifts from order to creating, sensing and building relationships.

Knowledge as an asset

In the past 50 years knowledge and intellectual assets have often been neglected, at a high cost. This negligence has extended to those managing human resource departments, for these managers may know how much the company spends on training, but they do not know how much *learning* has resulted from it. Knowledge is more than training people and this must be understood.

Equally, the accounts department can tell us the cost of material and labor, yet most products today consist largely of research and development, intellectual assets and services. Therefore we still have a way to go before individual or collective knowledge is 'valued'.

Until the thinking changes everywhere we each have to take responsibility for developing and expressing our knowledge. We can begin today. The starting point is to recognize that people know more than they realize. We store information, skills, intuition, mindsets, values we are not aware of, ways of working to a state of oblivion. If we can recall them, name them, put them together as we did earlier, we will have a store of tacit knowledge we can use that we didn't use yesterday.

How do you feel about the knowledge you have gained so far? Have you defined yourself as the person you always wanted to be or are you a 'work in progress'? Are you achieving your full potential as a knowledgeable human being? Or do you feel frustrated, incomplete or unfulfilled?

More knowledge

Using our knowledge capital is important for both individuals and organizations. Why is there a desire for more knowledge? Most of us are taught to believe that knowledge and truth are absolute and unchanging, and that we can discover what they are by asking the right people or looking up the appropriate reference. Yet developing knowledge about the world is a lifelong process of exploration that requires the use of all your human capital.

Exercise

Write down *all* the knowledge you have – explicit and tacit – on two of the following subjects.

1. Happiness.

2. The impact of technology on the Third World.

3. Personal development.

grow your personal capital

momentum

Read what you have written. Is there knowledge you weren't aware you had?

For a long time we have held so-called 'experts' – those we perceive as having the knowledge – in high esteem. That perception is beginning to crumble and a new one is developing – one that realizes that each one of us has valuable knowledge to be used at work. Beware, however, this realization is slow in reality and is usually misconceived as information rather than knowledge.

Knowledge and truth are goals we strive to achieve

Knowledge and truth are goals we strive to achieve, processes in which we are all actively involved as we construct our understanding of the world. And although the search for 'absolute knowledge' may be misconceived, we become wiser, more insightful and more knowledgeable about the world and the mysteries of life.

When you use your knowledge capital you can work out intuitively how to respond to shifting customer demands using the tools at your disposal. You can react to changing markets with freedom and motivation. When people are using all their knowledge they are happier at work. It is rigid management processes and hierarchical bureaucracies that stifle and constrain us. The most responsive system yet devised is the human system; its ability to respond to challenges is greater than any computer or man-made system – when it is allowed to do so.

Therefore to 'know' is more than gathering information, and knowledge is more than facts and figures. In fact, we will now see that knowledge capital is only the start of unravelling your human capital.

self-knowledge

To be an effective and whole human being you must have knowledge about who you are. It may seem a paradox, but to build healthy relationships with others you first need to have a positive relationship with yourself and it begins with self-knowledge.

You can look in the mirror and see yourself, but there is more of you that you will not see, hidden beneath like an iceberg. This knowledge is often forgotten, but in developing the whole human being, all your human capital, this knowledge is paramount. The aim of developing this knowledge is to be able to express your authentic self in everything you do.

Every human being on this planet is unique

Every human being on this planet is unique. Every human being is connected to all other life form on the planet. Every human being is made of stardust. Every atom in our bodies except for hydrogen began inside stars and scattered across the universe in stellar explosions, recycling to become part of you. Therefore we are all connected to the universe.

When we explore who we are we will find unique things about ourselves, but there are also processes that we all use to be a living, active human being. In helping you discover this knowledge as part of your human capital I would like to work around these processes while you use them to learn all about yourself and what is unique to you.

Exercise

The first step is to spend 10–15 minutes answering this question:

What sort of human being do you want to be?

Put down all the skills you would like and the character you want to be. It isn't an easy question to answer, but persevere and take as much time as you need to write as much as you can. This question is important.

Everything you have written down you already have the potential to be. It was the ancient Chinese writer Lao-tzu who said in the 6th century BC: 'At the centre of your being you have the answer; you know who you are and you know what you want.' This is the truth. We know who we are, the problem is we don't spend time learning this but instead focus on the world outside. Keep your exercise book at hand while you read this chapter. Learning about yourself requires reflection and takes time. But the payback is tenfold.

From the day we are born we receive information about the world and those around us. The first big influencers are our parents, then siblings, then friends, teachers and so on. All the information is filtered over the years through our language that we build up as a child. As this information grows we take on board beliefs and values. Very often these can be below our level of consciousness. These beliefs sometimes change as we grow up. Do you remember the day you found out there was no Santa Claus? I was about six and had been playing in the school playground when one of the older children told me. I remember how shocked I was and how difficult it was to accept this information as true. It was as if part of my world, part of my reality, had been removed.

Changing beliefs is not easy

Changing beliefs is not easy. Equally deep are the values that form the core of who you are. We are now going to explore the part of your human capital we call self-knowledge. Without this knowledge it is difficult to understand others and this will impact on your effectiveness at work as well as in your personal life.

Let's begin with how you perceive yourself right now.

Exercise

Answer this question: What is my current self-image? Write down how you see yourself in as much detail as possible. This can include your physical image, your health, your relationships, your hobbies and interests, yourself at work and the different roles you play in a day. Most of this writing will begin 'I am …'.

This is how you see yourself at this moment in time. When you have finished compare what you have just written with the answer you wrote for the question 'what sort of human being do you want to be?'. Is there a gap? How big is that gap? If the gap between how you perceive yourself and who you would like to be is large, you probably have an issue with self-esteem. What does this mean?

Self-esteem and self

Self-esteem is how you value yourself. If you perceive yourself as stupid, incapable or unworthy, everything you do will reflect this because inside you believe you are incapable or unworthy. When things get difficult at work, these feelings rise to the surface. The words you use around the workplace may give a different picture, but the reality will come out in your behaviour. This behaviour will lead to others behaving in a certain way towards you, thus reinforcing your low self-esteem. So if you believe you are incapable, the belief will come out in some of your actions at work and colleagues will start to perceive you as incapable and not include you in important, challenging projects. The good news is, you can change this.

Exercise

Go back to your exercise book and draw a vertical line down the center of the page. On one side write down the qualities you would like to develop in yourself more fully, such as trust, loving, optimistic, sensitive, open, secure, generous, flexible and so on. Keep going until you have listed all the qualities you would like to develop in yourself.

Then on the other side describe the qualities you would like to develop more fully in your relationships with others, such as empathetic, supportive, understanding and so on.

Finally, compare the two lists. What qualities are down for both yourself and others? Are there qualities on one list that on reflection you think should be on both? What is preventing you from being all these things? Write this down and look at it. How real is this block and are you going to continue living with it?

Often feelings of low self-esteem begin very young. If as a baby and child you felt with certainty that you were loved and valued, and that nothing could threaten this connection, you are likely to have a secure sense of yourself and who you are. You will see the world as a playground for adventure and will explore and try things with confidence.

Children and teenagers who get into trouble often have low self-esteem

On the other hand, like many people you may have suffered in some emotional way in childhood. This means that you may feel insecure and undeserving. The world is more likely to feel a scary place and your self-belief and confidence a mere varnish over what you really feel inside. Children and teenagers who get into trouble often have low self-esteem, usually because they do not feel wanted or loved. In fact, most of us are nearer the second scenario than the first. But we can overcome our negative beliefs by addressing the past, forgiving and moving on. When this happens we can be the parents we wish we'd had.

If you did have emotional experiences in childhood it is important to acknowledge and understand them.

Exercise

Describe your relationships with family members when you were growing up and how they have contributed to the person you are now. Did you feel valued? Did they show you trust? Did they show you love and affection? Write down your memories.

When you have done this, look for patterns – things that happen in your life now and in your life as a child. Once you have recognized these you have a choice – carry on repeating patterns or change them. So to finish, write down the actions you are going to take to change any patterns you choose to change and put a timescale on these.

What people seek

Now the focus can be on what it is you want. Abraham Maslow found that what people seek is:

◆ to be prime mover;

◆ self-determination;

◆ to have control over their fate;

- to determine their movements;

- to be able to plan and carry out and to succeed;

- to expect success;

- to like responsibility or at any rate to assume it willingly, especially for themselves;

- to be active rather than passive;

- to be a person rather than a thing;

- to experience themselves as the maker of their own decisions;

- autonomy;

- initiative;

- self-starting;

- to have others acknowledge their capabilities fairly.

This list has implications for the workplace, where lack of these has led to a build-up of stress as well as a lowering of self-esteem. Some organizations still treat individuals as cogs in the machine rather than as whole human beings. Go through the list and tick those that are most important to you. Do you have these at work? Developing your human capital may challenge your present situation and this is not something to be afraid of.

Maslow argues that dignity is at the heart of self-esteem and is easy to give people at work because it is a simple matter of attitude. For too long we have tried to 'fix' the people in organizations instead of which we should have been 'fixing' our organizations. What actions can you take to make work encompass the above list for yourself and your colleagues? Write them in your exercise book.

If, as Maslow says, the key to healthy self-esteem is to treat people with dignity, why is it so difficult for some individuals to do this? Our behaviour, including how we treat others, is strongly influenced by our beliefs and values. Remember the work of Douglas McGregor and his concepts of Theory X and Theory Y (*The Human Side of Enterprise*, McGraw Hill, 1960). These are not management 'styles' but assumptions based on beliefs. Theory X is based on the assumptions that people don't want to work, are lazy and need to be watched. These assumptions come from an individual's beliefs – something we keep coming back to.

Beliefs

Our beliefs shape what we do. Beliefs are views about ourselves, about others and about the world. We use them to understand the world and they come from our experience of life. We also use beliefs to make decisions and choices. Sometimes they are positive and sometimes negative. However, the bottom line is whatever we believe – is.

We also use beliefs to make decisions and choices

Exercise

Tomorrow you are going into work. Imagine your day and write it down. What does it look like? Is your day successful and fulfilling or frustrating with problems? These beliefs are deeply held in you and they are affecting your behaviour. I hear some say: 'This is all very well but my boss is the problem.' Have you ever thought that your beliefs about yourself and your boss are setting you up every day? You can't change your boss's behaviour, but you can change yours and by doing so the behaviour of your boss has to change.

The problem is we feel our beliefs are *the* truth and then form assumptions. Chris Argyris describes the process of forming these beliefs as a 'ladder of inference'. This is a mental pathway we follow that often results in misguided beliefs. The ladder takes the following form (see Figure 3.1):

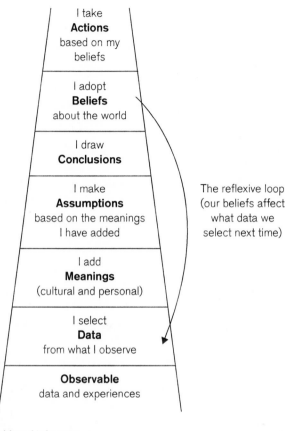

Figure 3.1 Ladder of inference

From Peter Senge et al., eds., *The Fifth Discipline Fieldbook* (1994) Currency/Doubleday

Step 1 Observable 'data' and experiences
Here an individual will capture data like a video recorder.

Step 2 Data
The individual then selects 'data' from the observation.

Step 3 Meanings
The individual adds meanings to the data that are influenced by
culture and personal understanding.

Step 4 Assumptions
The individual makes assumptions based on the meanings.

Step 5 Conclusions
The individual draws conclusions.

Step 6 Beliefs
The individual adopts beliefs about the world.

Step 7 Action
The individual takes actions based on their beliefs.

Argyris adds that our beliefs affect what data we select the next time. These assumptions lead to how we behave with people without being aware of their basis. The ladder of inference explains why most people don't usually realize where their deepest attitudes came from.

Exercise

Take an example from these:

… is unreliable/untrustworthy/lazy. Now work your way up the ladder.

When you have tried this use a real example from your experience. What was the outcome?

These emotionally held thoughts are based on our perception of events at the time they were formed – they can be changed.

Exercise

Write down two beliefs you have that hold you back – what can be called limiting beliefs. Examples can be 'I don't deserve success' or 'I can't do that sort of work'.

Now look into the future by five years and describe it as it is with these beliefs guiding you.

Stand up and, holding your head high, walk across the room and back. Now think of three beliefs that would change the future picture you have just described and write them down. Then describe your life in five years time living these new beliefs.

If you look at the two future pictures and study the words you will notice the first will contain words such as can't and won't be able, whereas in the second future view the words will be can, will and have. It is not only your beliefs that shape your behaviour – it's also the words you use.

Language

Each one of us experiences the world in a unique way. We use language to communicate but even the same language has 'problems'. The words we use have meaning through their association with objects and our experiences, and these will of course differ. Consider someone who works during the week saying they are having a day *unwinding*. This could mean sitting and reading a book and later watching a film. For another person it could mean doing some chores, cleaning the car and going for a long walk or having a game of tennis. For both the word unwinding will have very different meanings.

Language is a filter on our everyday experiences

Language is a filter on our everyday experiences. Language is cultural, as I found working with different nationalities. In our heads we have thoughts that are made up of mental models, feelings and sounds. We translate these into words through our language, but the meanings are often different.

What about in a work context? Two individuals will say: 'I empower my staff.' For one this will mean, I trust them implicitly and while I provide the direction they decide how to achieve the goals and implement their own plans. For another this will mean, I tell them what to do but then leave them to get on with it and they keep me informed on a weekly basis. Who would you rather work for?

Another issue with language and communication is that two people can describe the same event in two ways. For example, the company has just had a good conference. One person will return and say: 'That was great! The day went well and we have lots of new business leads from it.' Another person will say: 'The conference on e-commerce went really well, with each speaker showing a different aspect of the new business. The customers were delighted and we had 72 enquiries, of which 61 signed a contract.' The difference here is that the first person sees the world in 'big chunks' and the second sees the world in small, detailed chunks. The outcome is that they use language differently. Do you communicate in big pictures or in detail? You will inevitably prefer one, although you can move between the two.

Can you now see that even if we come from the same family and speak the same language, we will have our own ways of expressing ourselves? The important thing is that you are beginning to realize that developing your human capital is much more than learning some new skills! Self-knowledge is a huge area for development. So let's get back to you.

What drives you? What is important to you? Do you have this knowledge at your fingertips? The next part of your self-knowledge is your personal values.

Values

Values are deeply held views of what is important and worthwhile to us. Like beliefs they come from many sources, including parents, teachers, peers, individuals we admire and the culture we grow up in. There is a distinction between values we espouse to, vocalize in day-to-day conversation and profess to believe in; and those that guide our behaviour and so we can call them our values in action. These latter values are so deeply coded into us that we rarely question them. Consider the enticement of an affair or giving a competitor information about the company. Will you, won't you? What are the values that make up your self-knowledge?

Exercise

Here is a list of values that are part of both your personal and work life. Select from the list ten that you consider the most important to you. If you want to add any to the list, please do.

Achievement	Advancement
Adventure	Affection
Art	Balanced life
Change and variety	Close relationships
Competition	Creativity
Co-operation	Democracy
Decisiveness	Effectiveness
Ecological awareness	Ethical behaviour
Efficiency	Excitement
Excellence	Fame
Expertise	Fast pace
Family	Financial security
Financial gain	Friendships
Freedom	Helping others
Growth	Independence
Honesty	Inner harmony
Influencing others	Intellectual stimulation
Integrity	Job satisfaction
Involvement	Leadership
Knowledge	Loyalty
Learning	Meaningful work

Merit	Nature
Money	Order
Openness	Physical challenge
Personal development	Power
Pleasure	Public service
Privacy	Quality
Purity	Religion
Recognition	Responsibility and accountability
Reputation	Self-respect
Security	Spiritual growth
Sophistication	Time
Status	Truth
Tranquillity	Wisdom
Wealth	Work alone
Work with others	

Now cross off five so you have only five left. Then cross off two so you have only three. Take these three core values and one at a time remember when you had this value in what you were doing or feeling. Take the first one and when you remember, close your eyes and feel what it felt like. Then do the same for the other two. When you remember how it felt you will express these values in your daily life. It will also help you with the final stage of this exercise.

Cross off one of the values and choose between the last two the one which is the most important to you. When you identify your core values you signal to the world your true identity.

To act against our values will make us incongruent. As you get promoted within an organization you will need to adopt the organization's values. If they are different from your own it is likely to lead to incongruence. This is what happened to Nick in the story at the beginning of the book. It became more and more clear to him that the company values did not match his own until he found it intolerable to work there. The most lasting and influential of your values are freely chosen and you need to be aware of them in the knowledge of yourself. What would your organization have to ask you to get a negative response?

The most lasting and influential of your values are freely chosen

More self-knowledge requires you to recognize, explore and question deep inside yourself. All this questioning is building your self-knowledge, knowledge that is vital to you in developing your human capital. Other questions would include: 'Are you an extrovert or an introvert?'.

Extrovert or introvert

Have you noticed how some people walk into a room full of strangers and confidently say 'hello' to everyone while others walk in and say nothing? The difference is something we know as being an extrovert or an introvert.

Extroverts are confident in the world, will share their toys as children, enjoy parties and make friends easily. They love noise and will have New York or London as their favourite places. They need an audience and work things through by talking to others but lose interest quickly if they don't have the stimulus of other people around them. Extroverts do well in large companies where they remember people's names and they can become charismatic leaders.

Introverts have good concentration and enjoy reading and study. They are comfortable at parties when they know all the guests. They tend to have a small circle of trusted friends that they keep for a lifetime.

The truth is that no one is completely introvert or extrovert. But you will have a leaning towards one or the other. Here's a simple exercise to establish your preference. See which list you answer mostly 'yes' to.

1. You would rather have your own home than share it with lots of people.

2. You prefer parties where you know most of the guests.

3. You enjoy spending a quiet evening alone.

4. You prefer to plan ahead rather than to deal constantly with the unexpected.

5. You are modest about telling people your achievements.

6. People telephone you more than you telephone them.

7. You find it difficult to remember people's names.

8. You enjoy talking to people but it leaves you tired.

9. You are a good listener.

10. You find it easier to learn from books than being shown.

11. You prefer one-to-one discussions rather than addressing large groups.

12. You like having visitors but are usually relieved when they go home.

13. You are good at keeping secrets.

14. In a new group you prefer to let others take the lead.

1. People often choose you to run teams or organize events.

2. You like organizing events and making sure people have a good time.

3. You are full of ideas and projects for your friends and colleagues to carry out.

4. You like networking.

5. You are easily bored if you find yourself alone.

6. People sometimes think you tactless.

7. You like group vacations.

8. You frequently interrupt people and finish their sentences.

9. You enjoy doing new things.

10. You prefer newspapers and magazines to books.

11. You feel stimulated and energized by crowds.

12. You enjoy busy restaurants and crowded bars.

13. You hate to eat alone.

14. You are stimulated by crises and having to think on your feet.

If most yes answers were in the first list, you are more introvert; if most yes answers were from the second list, you are more extrovert. If you are an extrovert you will enjoy working in sales or marketing. If you are an introvert you are more likely to enjoy academic study that leads to medicine, law or technical work. The important thing is to recognize your preference because whatever your job, this preference will influence how you work and the relationships around you.

Two sides to being human

What else can you learn about yourself – your self-knowledge? According to ancient Chinese writings, every one of us has two sides, known as the yin and yang or often referred to as masculine and feminine. We all have some of both, but how can we use them? One of the best Chinese writers was Lao-tzu who wrote about powerful warriors and how they used their might to win battles. This he referred to as the yang or masculine side. He then referred to the yin or feminine side which he saw as being open, receptive and nourishing. He explained that the yin is like water while the yang is like rock. Water may yield and seem weaker than rock, yet it will wear away rock.

Every one of us has two sides

In trying to understand the yin and yang in ourselves you mustn't see the two parts as either/or because we are both yin and yang at the same time. Each part changes and grows as we live our life. The key is to 'feed' both at different times and not neglect one. I meet many women who work in a male environment who have developed their masculine side in order to be accepted and promoted. Then a crisis occurs and they realize that they have suppressed a part of themselves. Many leave at this point and take on totally different work to feed their feminine side again.

Exercise

To find your yin and yang, open your exercise book and draw a line down the middle of one page. Put the two headings at the top and list your characteristics under the relevant column. Is there a tendency to be more of one side than another? That is normal. What is important is to recognize both and develop both.

Another view on the two sides of a coin in self-awareness is the proposition given by Carl Jung. He believed that each of us has a Persona (who we appear to be) and an Ego (who we consciously think we are).

Persona and Ego

Persona is the image we present to the world. It includes the way we dress, how we speak and the personality that we like to project. This Persona is influenced by several factors, including our upbringing, culture, the media, advertisers, society norms and values that are perceived as desirable. The way we present ourselves informs people about us and helps them react to us.

The Persona is not the 'real me' but rather society's expectation

However, the Persona is not the 'real me' but rather society's expectation of how we should behave, dress, look and speak. In our profession we may be expected to be competent, in control, unemotional and rational. We play this role, but by doing so suppress other parts of our personality such as fun loving, creative, caring and passionate.

In young people today the pressure is on women to be slim and pretty while the men are expected to be muscular and 'hunky'. For those who don't fit this expectation the world can appear to be unfair and cruel.

Ego is what we believe we really are. It is our personality as we consciously know it and goes beyond what we do. It includes our driving force and our desire for self-expression. Ego is the Latin word for 'I' and we become aware of this 'I' in childhood.

The relevance of this information is that you need to recognize when you are in Persona and when you are in Ego for the two are different. Which are you in when meetings are difficult? In which situation does everything come together with ease when you are in Persona or Ego? When you demonstrate to the world a total congruence between who you are and what you say and do, you are expressing your authentic self and this is the aim of developing your self-awareness.

We cannot make healthy relationships unless we have a realistic sense of our own identity. When we feel secure within ourselves, we let those around us blossom and grow. If we are insecure we want control.

If we are insecure we want control

I worked with a company in which a director was known for not being easy to work for and upset those around him. He worked long hours and expected everyone else to do the same. He was brisk and aggressive and controlled the work in his area. It transpired that he was very insecure, having felt he 'failed' at school compared with his brother. He was living his working life as if to prove himself worthy to his father who had for years given him a negative view of himself. Developing Ego means letting go of the need for control, knowing who you are as a valued human being and seeing change and the unexpected as good.

Exercise

You can establish your Persona and your Ego. On a clean sheet draw a circle and write in the centre: What I like about myself. Think about those people who like and love you and what they might say about you and put these in the circle. Now think about what you might say about yourself. Write down all the positive qualities and characteristics in the circle.

When you have completed the first part go outside the circle and draw another circle. In the centre write: Myself as others would like me to be. See if you can name this image and draw it. There may be more than one image, so add these.

On another sheet of paper put the heading: Me as I would like to be perceived. Draw the image and write down any thoughts you have about it. If you can, it is a good idea to name it.

On a clean sheet draw a large circle and write in the centre: The image I present to the world. Look at what you have drawn and written – your positive image, the image others have of you and the 'real you'. Are there differences between them? Do you project yourself differently to others from the way you actually feel about yourself? What aspects of yourself are you hiding? Why are you hiding them? Are others' expectations limiting you in some way?

Finally, make a list of qualities that describe the way you present yourself to others. Compare it with the list of qualities that you wrote on your positive circle (the first one). What differences are there? Look at the image of the real you once more.

The final part of self-knowledge is self-acceptance. Accept who you are as a unique, beautiful, wondrous being who is intelligent, kind and loving. Use this part of your human capital in everything you do and you will become the best you can be.

grow your personal capital

momentum

chapter four
creative knowledge

What is creative knowledge? How creative are you? Have you asked yourself these questions lately? There is a tendency in society to perceive creativity as art, music, pottery, needlework or music. Therefore if an individual is not apparently 'talented' in any of these they are deemed not to be creative. Is this right? Being creative is a state of mind and as such is open to everyone. Whenever you think of unique ideas you are being creative.

According to Abraham Maslow, creativity is inherent in all human beings. This is reiterated by Ned Herrmann, founder of Whole Brain Technology and pioneer of creative thinking, who found creativity a mental process and therefore within everyone's reach. But what is this process of being creative? Can you tap into it? What is your creative knowledge potential? Creative knowledge means bringing your unique ideas and perspective and creative talents to all the dimensions of your life. When you do this, you bring a richer, more productive approach to everything you do. However, although we all have this potential, most people use only a fraction of their creative knowledge.

What is your creative knowledge potential?

Maslow was in fact one of the best writers on creativity and was a remarkably futuristic thinker as his work, written during the 1960s, is more relevant today than ever before. He viewed creativity as a holistic part of the human being and believed that studying art education didn't just turn out artists, but more importantly, better people.

Today we hear a great deal about a changing world, yet Maslow saw transformation in the world decades earlier and the need for people who transformed with the world. He wrote:

'... what I'm talking about is the job of trying to make ourselves over into people who don't need to staticize the world, who don't want to freeze it and make it stable ... who are able confidently to face tomorrow not knowing what's going to come, not knowing what will happen, with confidence enough in ourselves that we will be able to improvise in that situation which has never existed before.'

(*The Farther Reaches of Human Nature*, Penguin Books, 1993)

Maslow set about studying the process of creativity which he saw as vital for individuals dealing with a fast-changing world. One of his first 'discoveries' was that individuals in the inspirational phase lose the past and future and live only in the moment. He wrote: 'The ability to become "lost in the present" seems to be a *sine qua non* for creativeness of any kind' (*The Farther Reaches of Human Nature*).

Have you experienced this feeling of being so engrossed you are living for the moment? That is when you are expressing your creativity. Think of that situation now and remember how it felt. Use words to describe it in your exercise book.

Living for the moment

Would you agree it is a powerful experience that energizes rather than drains the individual? How can you tap into this? The first requirement is to understand and recognize this place of being in the present. According to Maslow, while in this phase the individual behaves in a kind of 'innocent' way, acting without any *a priori* expectation, without dogma or idea of what is proper.

Children are the best at this and I believe we can achieve this 'innocence' by 'behaving' in a childlike manner for a short time to capture creativity, for example, sitting on the floor, cutting pictures out of magazines and making a collage. At work, we sit at desks attending uncreative meetings followed by writing up boring reports and plans. We forget how good it feels to connect to 'our child' and be creative. Becoming 'child-like' is not the same as 'childish'. Child-like behaviour allows us to get rid of the rules, labels, images and so on that stifle the creativity within us.

Child-like behavior allows us to get rid of the rules

If we can achieve this state we also become less conscious of everything except the matter in hand – another criterion for Maslow. We forget to act out our Persona; we stop worrying about what we look like to others, and about their expectations. We stop trying to influence, impress, to please, or to win applause. Maslow explains this superbly when he writes: 'This is because *the* greatest cause of our alienation from our real selves is our neurotic involvements with other people, the historical hangovers from our childhood, the irrational transferences, in which past and present are confused, and in which the adult acts like a child' (*The Farther Reaches of Human Nature*).

In becoming totally absorbed we become less conscious of ourselves and instead more open, more unifying and integrated as a person. We also become less judgemental and critical. In this way we are being not only creative but more authentic, more our real selves, and thus we tend to become more positive and don't reject or disapprove.

The importance of trust

The most important part of this creative process is that we develop a sort of trust in ourselves and in the universe and give up striving and controlling while we are in this 'live for the moment', creative place. Maslow saw trust as fundamental in dealing with novelty and transformation in the future. In this way trust involves self-confidence, courage and lack of fear of the world. In fact, fear and weakness limit creativity.

Creativity enriches life in many ways

Creativity enriches life in many ways, bringing a harmonious balance as well as self-actualization. It is also therapeutic and relaxing. Just as you cannot rush a painting, you cannot rush around an art gallery. To live creatively is to live with freedom away from day-to-day pressures.

For Maslow, creativity was a quality of the whole person and not added to the person through teaching. Instead the person and the world become fused. In organizations today can you unleash this creativity? To enable people at work to be fully creative involves taking risks – there are likely to be mistakes, broken rules and a challenge to the status quo. Those at the top of organizations who say they want to tap into the creativity around them often want the fruits of creativity but not the challenges to the status quo.

At the same time, managers try to manage and control creativity. This approach is effective only if organizations want to inhibit the flow. You cannot be rational about creativity – there has to be freedom to imagine what is possible. When Albert Einstein was working on one of his theories he would imagine himself riding a light wave. It was through this imagination that he was able to advance our understanding of the world.

Exercise

Here's an exercise to do over the weekend. It sounds a bit childish, but the results may surprise you.

Gather as many magazines and Sunday supplements as you can find. Put them on the floor with a pair of scissors, a *large* piece of paper and paper glue. Go through the magazines and look for pictures that you are attracted to – don't spend time analyzing this, just tear out the ones you like. Then make a collage of the pictures by cutting them up and putting them on the large sheet as you wish. When you have finished, sit cross-legged on the floor and tell yourself the collage is you. It is a representation of yourself. Look at the pictures and tell yourself how these pictures represent who you are. You will find that the collage will describe you – this is the power of your inner creative potential and why you should use it as part of your human capital.

Creative knowledge involves experiment, playing, working with ideas to enable you to look at something and see something else, making connections between things and seeing possibilities. Fundamental to the creative process is to think and see 'outside the box' and there are three creative ways to do this.

Ways to be creative

The first is brainstorming, a method used since the 1960s but often not as it should be. The process involves getting together a group of people who offer different perspectives and generating as many ideas as possible. One person should be recording them as they jump out.

The group need to follow two rules only: the first is to keep ideas flowing and not begin discussing any of them; the second is to agree that any idea that is relevant, no matter how bizarre or ridiculous, should be included. These two rules ensure that ideas are not judged or stifled as this discourages people to be fully creative. Another important point is to do the activity either standing around a flip chart or, even better, sitting on the floor. Sitting around a board table immediately puts up a barrier and people behave 'sensibly'. Evaluation comes later, after the ideas have stopped flowing.

This method can also be used by one person to develop creative potential. So let's try out your creative intelligence using brainstorming.

Exercise

Put your watch on the table beside you. In one minute write down all the uses you can possibly think of for a paperclip. How many did you come up with? If you listed more than six then you have good creative knowledge.

The second method is to create mind maps. This is a process that can be used on your own or with a small group. It is a good way to capture a large number of ideas incorporating colour, dimensions and visual images as well as words (see Figure 4.1). You begin your mind map by writing the main subject in the centre of a page and then record all the ideas that you can relate to the subject by using connecting lines. You can draw pictures or use words. Clusters will form and these should be in different colours.

The value in using this method is to let your mind run freely and work as quickly as possible. Let the map grow naturally, reflecting the way your mind makes associations and connections and organizes information.

Exercise

Think of a subject or topic close to your heart. Using a double page put your subject in the center, overlapping the two pages. Take a pack of colored pens and just go. It really is fun and productive.

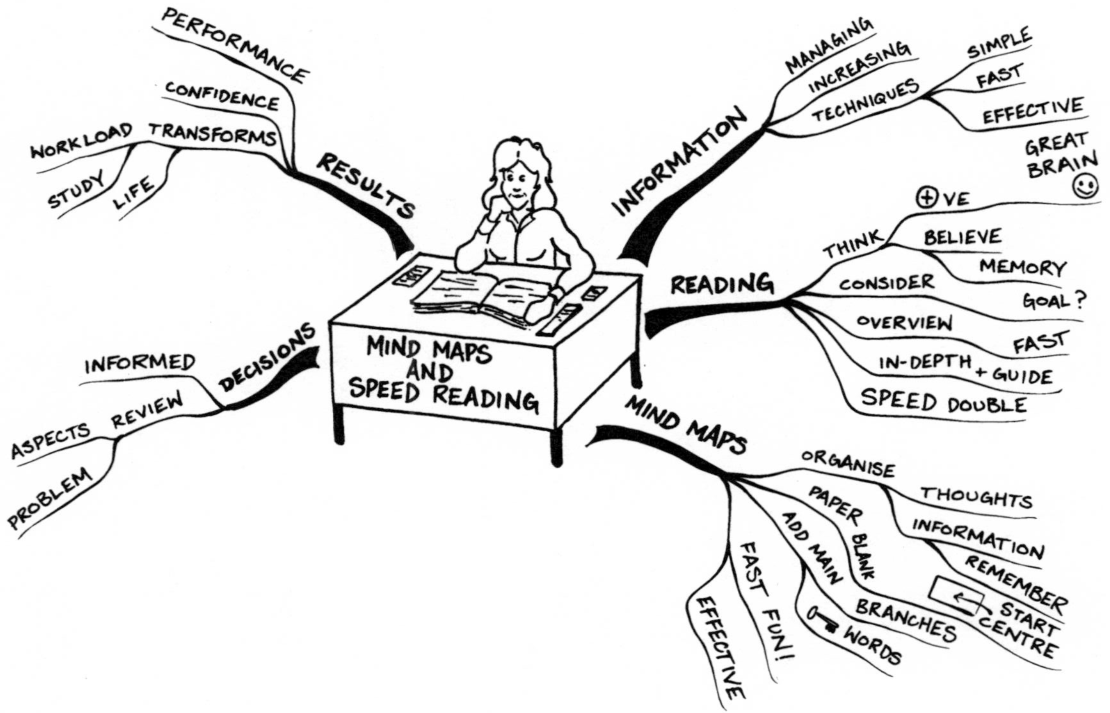

Figure 4.1 A mind map (© Helen Whitten)

The third method to tap your creative knowledge is dreamwork. Dreams contain more than just our conscious awareness of events; they are an expression of our deeper mental processes and emotions. They often have vivid images and thus are a route to our deep creative knowledge.

The only drawback is that we forget them very quickly, so you need to record your dreams as soon as you wake in the mornings – keep a notebook beside your bed. When you have described the dream you then use your imagination to try to interpret it. Carl Jung used dreamwork as a creative process to access material from the unconscious. In analyzing your dreams look for patterns. The point to remember is that most dreams are triggered by incidents the day before.

Tapping into your creativity

So why do people create? It seems to follow a process of tapping into oneself and then expressing to the world what lies within – the spirit or soul saying 'I am unique'. We can call this your 'essence', the most important feature that determines your unique identity. Tapping into your creative capital involves living from this essence where your creative impulses come forth.

How about turning one of the meeting rooms in your building into a play room with wooden bricks, play dough, paint and paper, magazines, scissors, glue etc. This will instantly stimulate creativity (and you never know, meetings may be quite enjoyable).

Creative intelligence is part of your human capital

Creative intelligence is part of your human capital and needs to be developed. We also need to feed our creativity with music, art, nature and so on. When you start developing your creative intelligence you will begin to notice all the creativity around you and begin to connect with it.

Exercise

Answer the following question:

How can creativity improve my life?

What actions am I going to take to have more creativity in my work? Put a timescale on this to review.

chapter five
inner wisdom

It must be becoming clear now that developing your human capital involves a journey that takes you deeper and deeper into your core being. Since the Industrial Revolution employers and managers have seen human beings as a resource – a body that has skills to achieve work goals. When treated this way, it is difficult to perceive people as any different to that view.

Today, a growing consciousness is dawning that as human beings we have much more than skills. There has been talk of knowledge assets, but even this is a limited view of what people bring to work. In the previous chapter we explored creative knowledge that comes from the essence of who we are. In addition, we said that this capability is there in everyone, which led Maslow to write: 'The key question isn't "what fosters creativity?" But it is why in God's name isn't everyone creative? Where was the human potential lost? How was it crippled? I think therefore a good question might be not why do people create? But why do people not create or innovate?' (*The Farther Reaches of Human Nature*).

From early childhood we develop logic and reasoning skills to deal with the world. In other words we learn to think rather than feel our way through life. Does it matter? Yes, when we have neglected our creativity and other forms of knowledge, although that does not mean we want to open up a flood-gate to emotions and stop thinking logically and rationally. The message from this book is that we need to develop the whole human being – all our human capital.

In this chapter we explore a form of knowledge which we all have and which we can all tap into. In developing rational, logical, analytical, reasoning skills we are using only half our brain – the left side – and neglecting the potential of the right side of the brain. The intuition, emotional intelligence and inner knowledge of just 'knowing' have been discarded, undervalued and largely unused. Yet we have an inner wisdom that is probably superior to the capabilities of the left-brain knowledge.

We have an inner wisdom

Once you can accept the potential of your subconscious mind, understand how it works and discover how to use it, you will have additional knowledge that I prefer to call 'wisdom'. This wisdom is different to knowledge in that you have to be still and listen for it rather than seek it in a book or lecture. This wisdom will provide guidance, clarity, protection and a sense of 'knowing' what is truth. The problem is, we don't always trust this wisdom. So the first step is to understand it.

Developing right-brain activity

Intuition and emotions come from the right side of the brain. Intuitive feelings are related to but different from emotional feelings. How do you recognize intuition? Recall a time when you had a hunch or feeling about something and you followed your intuition. What was the outcome? Now recall a time when you had an intuitive feeling but you didn't follow it. What was the outcome? Finally, think of a situation where you were faced with decisions and people offered you some guidance that didn't fit with your intuitive feelings. Which did you listen to and trust the most? Would you do the same today?

Instead of analyzing intuition we need to understand it as the ability to access deep into our subconscious mind, the recesses of which we are unaware. Therefore to use this knowledge we have to listen and feel rather than think. The problem is that logic can often get in the way, so to access intuition we have to 'let go' of the logical part of the brain.

When I'm in a new place, perhaps trying to find the offices of a new client, the road signs sometimes stop and I suddenly feel lost. These days I let go of any logic and 'feel' my way to where I need to be. This works about 99 per cent of the time, and when it doesn't logic has interfered. Writing this sounds bizarre but believe me, it really does work. When you trust your intuition and instincts you tap into an inner guidance or wisdom that provides opportunities that would otherwise lay dormant. Intuition serves inspiration. It is the sudden answer that appears from nowhere. This tends to happen when we go to sleep with a problem on our mind. In the morning, as we are waking, the answer comes to us in a flash. To increase this wisdom you can try asking for the answer before going to sleep, thereby bringing intention into play.

Intuition serves inspiration

In addition to this knowledge there is an inner wisdom that enables you to know something without having proof or evidence – you just know. Carl Jung called this 'the universal unconsciousness'. He saw it as a storehouse of inherited instincts and universal ideas of humankind that have evolved over the millions of years of human existence.

The universal unconsciousness

At this moment in time there is a fast-growing universal 'unconsciousness' about how we see the world and ourselves in it. Once you become part of it you keep bumping into people who are also aware of this new paradigm emerging. What is this 'knowing' which is emerging collectively?

It revolves around seeing the world as an interconnected place where human beings and all life are connected rather than isolated. It is based on the recognition that we are more than just bodies functioning to propagate a life form but are here to learn and experience life in this form to evolve our spirit to be all that it can become. When we understand this we can trust this inner wisdom because we know the universe is not the violent place we have made it but rather a place of compassion and love where we can be and become. When we really understand this we find an inner peace.

How do we tap into this inner wisdom? By being quiet. We all rush around, never having time to just be quiet, but to tap into this inner wisdom you have to find time at least once a week to sit quietly and hear the inner wisdom. Ideally, every morning before you get up it is really effective to sit in total silence for five minutes with your eyes closed and just become one with the quiet.

Sit up in bed with your pillows propped up behind you. Close your eyes and relax your hands in your lap. Breathe slowly in and then out. Keep breathing and listen to it. Then think of your day and what you would like to achieve. See yourself doing this and feel how at the end of the day you have achieved what you set out to do. Open your eyes and write down what you saw yourself doing. Then get up and prepare yourself for the day ahead. If you do this on a regular basis you will find yourself achieving the days you hope for. You will also be in the right frame of mind for the day to use all your knowledge at work.

Being a knowledge worker does not just mean being up to speed on technology or studying a subject in depth, it also means accepting that there is a knowledge that comes from inside when we make time to listen. This source of knowledge is attuned to your body and can surprise you at times. Have you noticed how you sometimes wake up just before the alarm goes off? Or sometimes you know the phone is going to ring just before it does – sometimes you even know who is phoning! This is normal and shouldn't surprise us.

There is a knowledge that comes from inside

Exercise

List similar events that demonstrate this inner knowledge. Did they surprise you? Do you trust this knowledge?

Inner wisdom is part of your human capital and the way to use it is to make time to be quiet. Dan Millman, author of *No Ordinary Moments A Peaceful Warriors Guide to Daily Life*, H.J. Kramer Inc., 1992, tells a story of the teachings on Hawaii which is worth thinking about. The story is about natives who had not been exposed to pure scientific, rational thought that dominated Europe. Instead they developed knowledge from their whole brain, including this inner knowledge. These people believed that when the soul is born in a physical body, it has with it three selves: a higher self (or guardian angel); a basic self (the subconscious mind and instinctive body wisdom); and a conscious self (or ego identity that develops as we grow out of infancy).

The story goes that the higher self can communicate to you only through your basic self (subconscious) through your body and senses. The better attuned you are to your physical senses and emotions, the better you can see, feel, hear the guidance of your higher self. What is interesting is that Jung also came up with three layers of being human – the Persona (what we project), the Ego (who we are) and the eternal Self (a deeper, wiser being), therefore showing that much of the knowledge we have is already within us – we just need to listen to it.

Listening

Learning to trust your instinct and intuition means listening to your inner wisdom. How can you do this? One of the best ways is through simple meditation. It takes time and practice to really meditate, but even a simple meditation is beneficial. As you are reading this book you must be relaxed. So follow these simple instructions and you can try a simple meditation. Read the instructions first, then follow them.

Sit in a comfortable chair, on the end of your bed or cross-legged on the floor. Rest your hands in your lap and close your eyes. Breathe slowly and listen to your breathing … Clear your mind of all thoughts and concentrate on your breathing. After a few moments imagine a warm, golden light around you. Let the light shine all around you. Feel its warmth. Stay there for as long as you want and when you open your eyes write down how you feel. The longer you stay, the more the benefit at this stage. When you have done this a couple of times try asking for guidance in a problem/issue you are facing just before you switch your mind off and focus on the breathing. At some point during the day or night the answer will come.

The biggest kept secret in the world, I believe, is that inside us is an abundance of wisdom and knowledge that only a few realize. In developing our human capital, each aspect must be acknowledged and understood. In addition, just as there are technologies to develop the analytical side of the brain, there are techniques to help develop the intuitive side.

The first step is to free yourself of negative emotions that will block your ability to feel and listen to your inner wisdom. Finding the right life coach or mentor can help you achieve this. The second step is to approach developing your inner wisdom with an open heart and mind.

Approach developing your inner wisdom with an open heart and mind

So how can you use your inner wisdom and practise this part of your human capital? Here is an exercise Dan Millman uses and it is really effective.

You are in a situation when you have to decide between three options: A, B and C.

Let's assume you opt for A. Now sit quietly with your eyes closed, take a deep breath and relax. Ask yourself the following questions and see what happens in your mind:

Having chosen A, what will I look like, feel like and be doing one hour from now? (Let your intuitive imagination create a picture.)

Having chosen A, what will I look like, feel like and be doing one day from now? (Again wait and see.)

Having chosen A, what will I look like, feel like and be doing one week from now? (Wait and see.)

Having chosen A, what will I look like, feel like and be doing one year from now? (Wait.)

Having chosen A, what will I look like, feel like and be doing ten years from now? (Wait.)

Then go through the same list for choices B and C. At the end of the process, you will have gained a better insight and perspective for an important decision. Your intuition has helped you.

In developing your inner wisdom you have a resource you can use in many aspects of your life and it will help you become the best you can be because that is why it was given to you. There is so much of our human capital we do not use, especially at work where we spend so much of our time. The thing to remember about all your human capital is that it needs to be used. The more you use all this potential, the better you will become. The key is not to dismiss any of the aspects that make up your human capital.

chapter six
world knowledge

We now focus on your knowledge of the outside world. Your human capital requires you to develop your knowledge of both the inner and the outer world. Each of us has a picture of 'reality' or how we see the world. This view has been shaped by our childhood, growing up, the media and our constant interaction within it. The pictures we carry with us today are different to how we saw reality years ago. This shifting reality of the world demonstrates that the reality we see is shaped by our beliefs and understanding.

Even in the last 50 years our collective view of the world has changed with pictures of our planet from space – a beautiful blue globe in a vast black universe. Sometimes our understanding of the world is so dramatically changed it is called a 'paradigm shift', a concept first used by Thomas Kuhn, a philosopher and science historian. A paradigm is a worldview and in science this means that the scientific community have a 'worldview' of how they see reality. Kuhn explained: 'Paradigms change … cause scientists to see the world of the research-engagement differently. In so far as their only recourse to that world is through what they see and do, we may want to say that after a (scientific) revolution, scientists are responding to a different world' (*The Structure of Scientific Revolutions*, University of Chicago Press, 1962).

A paradigm is a worldview

As a political scientist I found that individuals were influenced in their knowledge and understanding of the world by the newspaper they read, showing the bias of information we receive every day.

Exercise

Take a large piece of paper. At the top write 'The World'. Then spend 5–10 minutes using pictures and words to outline your vision of the world today as you see it and put yourself in it. It is really important that you do this exercise. We will come back to it.

Our world knowledge is an important part of developing human capital because it affects our view of ourselves. In Ancient Egypt the people believed that if they worked to build a tomb for the Pharaoh so he could pass safely to eternity, they would also have a place in the next world. The Egyptian world was based on *maat*, the principle of order and hierarchy. No one questioned the uneven distribution of wealth, status or the right to rule. In return, stability was maintained for the majority where world knowledge was based on knowing one's place in it. This regime lasted for thousands of years.

The world knowledge of Ancient Greece still influences us today. More than 2000 years ago there were arguments that have echoed down the ages. Parmenides of Elea in southern Italy argued that in the world 'nothing changes', whereas Heraclitus of Ephesus in Asia Minor said that 'all is flux'. This old world knowledge included the notion of the world being made up of tiny parts called atoms that were invisible and were of different sizes and shapes with a void between them.

Aristotle has probably had the greatest influence on our world knowledge. His explanations of much of physics, logic, economics, psychology, metaphysics, meteorology and ethics lasted for more than 1000 years. He categorized life forms and placed men at the top of the hierarchy, with women below. The Greeks' knowledge had a huge impact on our understanding of the world and our place in it for many centuries.

Growing understanding

Our understanding of world knowledge grew with individuals such as the astronomers Ptolemy, Copernicus and Kepler. Ptolemy believed our world was the center of the universe and the Church incorporated this into its view of the world. Copernicus put the sun at the centre of the universe, then one of his followers, Kepler, challenged much of our past world knowledge. Like Pythagoras, the Greek philosopher and mathematician, Kepler saw pattern in everything and using mathematics he showed that planets move in ellipses, not circles as Copernicus had thought, and that their motions are faster in some parts of their orbit than in others. This destroyed the Ancient Greeks' belief that all celestial movements must make symmetrical patterns. However, another genius was to transform our world knowledge.

Another genius was to transform our world knowledge

Galileo was a professor of mathematics in Italy who discovered the laws of falling bodies or laws of motion. Using the best of the telescopes he had made, he studied shadows on Venus and from their changing patterns deduced that Venus was orbiting the sun, thus making the sun the center of our universe. This world knowledge was a serious threat to the Church which still wanted to believe that we were the center of the universe. Galileo was made a prisoner for the rest of his life by order of the Church.

His contribution to world knowledge includes the principle of the pendulum that transformed the accuracy and manufacture of clocks. Galileo also showed that any body, no matter how heavy, falls at the same velocity. He discovered that heavenly bodies do not move naturally in circles or ellipses, but in a straight line unless some other force acts upon them. Yet he could not understand how we did not fall off the earth. Someone else was to fathom this and add it to our world knowledge.

Isaac Newton was born the year after Galileo died. By combining Kepler's laws of planetary motion and Galileo's laws of falling bodies (adding gravity), Newton formulated the general laws of motion governing all objects in the solar system and in doing so completed the work of Kepler, Copernicus and Galileo. The Church also accepted this knowledge and a worldview of a machine universe emerged. As such it justified the notion that as human beings we were the masters of nature, thus laying the foundations for the Industrial Revolution. What is striking throughout this quick history of our understanding of the world is how our world knowledge has such an impact on our lives.

With a machine scientific worldview it became more and more difficult to believe in a god, and a spiritual vacuum began to grow. There was no room for purpose or spirit. Instead the rational approach to human issues became paramount and we entered what came to be known as the Age of Enlightenment.

Another huge paradigm was emerging – that of evolution. It was the biologist Jean Baptiste Lamark who first turned the hierarchy upside down by saying that we all evolved from simple life. Several decades later, Darwin presented the evidence to support biological evolution in his *Origin of the Species*, published in 1859. Our view of the world was once again trying to absorb this revolutionary thinking on world knowledge. Yet before Darwin's famous publication, Herbert Spencer was the first by a decade to bring the ideas of evolution into Victorian society. It was Spencer who used the phrase 'survival of the fittest' and this world knowledge was most warmly received in the US where the 'fittest' were to become millionaires.

Darwin's contribution was to give us 'a place in the world, not as conquerors with spoils but as inheritors with responsibilities' (Brian Silver, *The Ascent of Science*, OUP, 1998). Some of this thinking was reflected in the writings of Charles Dickens and William Blake, both of whom saw the cruel side to evolution and the need for social reform.

Modern knowledge

By the end of the 19th century, evolutionary thinking had spread to physics where Max Planck was developing thermodynamics, or the science of heat. Through his experiments Planck discovered that energy is emitted not as a continuum but in discrete units, or quanta.

In biology, evolution meant a movement towards increasing order and complexity; in physics, because of thermodynamics, it came to mean the opposite, a movement towards increasing disorder. Another paradigm shift in our world knowledge was about to occur.

The exploration of the atomic and sub-atomic world brought scientists into contact with a strange and unexpected reality that shattered the foundations of their worldview and forced them to think in entirely new ways. Revolutions such as those of Copernicus and Darwin had introduced profound changes in the general conception of the universe and our world knowledge, changes that shocked many people, but the new concepts themselves were not too difficult to grasp. This time, at the beginning of the 20th century, scientists faced a serious challenge to their ability to understand the world and reality.

Scientists faced a serious challenge

Every time they asked nature a question in an atomic experiment, nature answered with a paradox, and the more they tried to clarify the situation, the sharper the paradoxes became. In their struggle to grasp this new reality, scientists became painfully aware that their basic concepts, their language and their way of thinking, were inadequate to describe atomic phenomena. Their challenge now wasn't only intellectual, it was emotional and existential and required fundamental transformation.

Beginning with Einstein, colleagues such as Heisenberg, Bohr and Schrodinger found it necessary to change their concepts of space, time, matter, object, cause and effect – in other words, reality itself. From this emerged quantum theory or quantum mechanics. Einstein turned Newton's notion of gravity upside down and produced his general theory of relativity.

From this work came a different worldview. The universe was no longer a machine made up of objects but dynamic, holistic, organic, interrelated and understood as patterns of a cosmic process. For atoms turned out not to be solid particles but rather vast regions of space in which extremely small particles, electrons, moved around the nucleus. They had a dual nature, sometimes seen as particles, sometimes as waves.

Uncertain world

In Newton's physics the world consisted of tiny particles that bumped into, attracted or repelled each other. They were solid and separate, each occupying its own place in space and time. Wave motions were not considered fundamental things. In quantum physics, however, both waves and particles are fundamental because each is a way in which matter can manifest itself yet we can never focus on both at the same time.

Later it was possible to deal with even the sub-atomic level and there it was found that matter does not exist with certainty at definite places but rather shows 'tendencies to exist'. In addition, atomic events do not occur with certainty at definite times and in definite ways, but show 'tendencies to occur'. This meant that the world knowledge of a determined reality which Newton had expressed was replaced with a world of interconnections and relationships.

This new world knowledge is now everywhere we look. Globalization, the Internet, connecting with customers, connecting with each other and our planet are all part of this new world knowledge of reality. Look at the picture you drew. Is it made of separate parts or are they interconnected? This will tell you where you are in your perception of world knowledge.

What does this mean for you in developing your human capital? It means you need to develop your world knowledge because it will affect how you operate in the world.

For a long time now we have lived with the machine-like world reality

For a long time now we have lived with the machine-like world reality of the Industrial Age, leading to individuals feeling isolated, alone and unloved. At work most organizations are still engrossed in this world knowledge and treat people as resources rather than intelligent, creative, innovative beings. In the 'old' world knowledge there is the requirement for order and control and this is provided by management. Organizations themselves are perceived as machines with parts that need constant monitoring.

To develop your human capital you need to understand the new world knowledge and leave behind the old worldview. Our world in the 21st century is not about solid objects we control but rather forms that come into being and are observed only in relationship to something else. Our world is made up of interconnected energy forces where relationships and trust replace order and control. German physicist Werner Karl Heisenberg said: 'The world thus appears as a complicated tissue of events, in which connections of different kinds alternate or overlap or combine and thereby determine the texture of the whole.'

For thousands of years, people have been trying to understand their relationship to the rest of the universe. In this new understanding of world knowledge you are not isolated and alone. Each of us is connected to others and to all life. In fact, the elements that make us, come from stars, thus showing that we are even connected to the universe as a natural product of it.

World of chaos

Instead of determined reality scientists studying chaos have found a different world, adding yet another shift in our world knowledge. One of these scientists, James Gleick, wrote: 'Relativity eliminated the Newtonian illusion of absolute space and time; quantum theory eliminated the Newtonian dream of a controllable measurement process; and chaos eliminates the Laplacian fantasy of deterministic predictability' (*Chaos*, Viking, 1987). Yet some people still write business plans believing a predictable future.

In the old world knowledge there is an assumption that our universe has order and laws of nature that we simply need to identify. Many of these laws we learned at school. The focus for scientists was to find order. This goal has extended into our organizations through management.

In the 1990s a handful of mathematicians, physicists, biologists and chemists began to find their way through disorder and irregularity. Today when we look we find chaos everywhere around us. We may not like it, but this includes where we work. Start looking for chaos in your organization.

Chaotic systems are characterized by extreme sensitivity to initial conditions. Over a period of time, minute changes will lead to large-scale consequences. In chaos theory this is known as the 'butterfly effect', based on the widely known idea of a butterfly that stirs the air today in Beijing causing a hurricane in New York next month. As an individual living and working in a world of chaos there is a need for flexibility, adaptability and self-belief as an intelligent, creative person who can respond (not react) to chaotic happenings around us. Therefore, in order to develop our human capital, we need to become more flexible and adaptable to be able to respond in an intelligent way.

This leads to a *big* question: has the world changed? Is it more chaotic than ever before? The short answer is that our perception of the world has changed. Therefore the development of your human capital needs to be different. It is no longer a case that you go to work and do a job that requires a skill. Today the emphasis is on developing your full human capital potential and this chapter shows more than any of the others why this full potential is needed.

Simple vs complex

Before our world knowledge included chaos theory the expectation was that simple systems behaved in simple ways, while complex systems behaved in complex ways. In the new world knowledge it has been found that simple systems give rise to complex behaviour and complex systems give rise to simple behaviour. Yet we still assume that a large organization will be more complex than a small business and is therefore more difficult to change. This assumption is not true in fact.

Therefore, all in all our world knowledge is an important factor in developing our human capital. It impacts particularly on how we see the world and from that, how we relate to this knowledge and understanding. Before you move on to the next chapter it is worth repeating the exercise you did at the beginning of this chapter. Draw the world as you now understand it. Is it different after reading this? How? Is learning more about knowledge one of the changes you are going to make after reading this book? It is a fascinating area to develop your human capital.

03

part three
social capital

chapter seven
making connections

Following on from the previous chapter the world we now 'know' is one of interconnections and this has new meaning for people who want to become the best they can be. It was through the study of ecology that life was clearly seen to be not about hierarchies but about networks.

At work we operate through the relationships we have with other people. An organization shouldn't be a structure but a community of relationships. Successful organizations are aware of the multiple relationships among its members and this gives a sustainable community. Nourishing the community means nourishing those relationships. When an individual is truly connected to an organization they become connected to something deep inside themselves, to the desire to contribute through meaningful work and to feel part of a greater whole.

During the 1980s there was a surge in 'networking'. We all joined networks of professional bodies meeting for breakfast, lunch or evening functions. The emphasis was on 'selling' ourselves and our business. This worked for a while, especially for those who were good at selling. Then what happened?

Networks and entrepreneurs

The 1980s saw a rise in women's networks such as the London-based City Women's Network. These networks consisted of women working in the City and the professions such as law and public relations, and aimed to give support to women breaking into male-dominated environments. Similar local networks were set up around the UK, again offering support and empathy for women in the professions.

The entrepreneurs were different from their corporate counterparts

Also during the 1980s entrepreneurship came into its own and women entrepreneurs made up a growing number of these networks. The entrepreneurs were different from their corporate counterparts and professional colleagues in that getting business was more important to them than support or empathy. Their main focus in joining networks was to gain business from other women. Over time, however, this drove away many of the corporate women because they felt attending meetings or events meant 'being sold to'. Eventually the entrepreneurs moved on and most of the networks collapsed.

Around the same time came a rise in business breakfast meetings which attracted lots of people because they didn't interrupt the busy day. Again, the networks were popular at first and people made friends and learned from the speakers. But after a while word spread and these networks filled up with insurance salespeople, estate agents, car salespeople, bankers looking for new business, and so on. The emphasis again changed to selling and many left. This 'hard' networking with its emphasis on *selling* is now being replaced with 'knowledge' networking where the emphasis is on *information* and personal growth.

In May 2000 the Institute of Leadership was launched in the UK. The institute is a not-for-profit, independent global organization with an emphasis on research, information, knowledge, innovative, forward-thinking development of individuals, projects to challenge and change people's thinking, and a growing network of people who want to learn more about leadership for themselves and others. At the first membership forum of founder members the participants were asked what they wanted from the organization. The answer came back: learning, knowledge, personal growth and connecting with others.

So how can you make connections as part of developing your human capital?

Exercise

The first step is to identify what is important to you. To some extent you did this in Chapter 3 when you discovered your key values. Have a look at them again and ask questions such as: what do I need to do to have this in my life? Who can help me? Where can I get the information? What organizations are out there to help me learn? What is stopping me from having this in my life? What are the steps I need to take to start from today to put this important learning in my life? Write down your answers because we are going to link all this up in the final chapter.

Finding common ground

To build connections you need to establish common ground with others, either within your organization or outside, or both. Internal networking is successful when those inside an organization have had a similar learning experience. If some of you have recently been on a development program, the outcome is far more effective when the group maintain the connections and meet on a regular basis.

What prevents us from making connections? There seem to be two barriers: time and a culture of individualism. Time is a rare commodity in modern life. For most people the priority is:

1. work

2. partner and family

3. mundane everyday chores

4. social life

5. ourselves.

How do we feel about this? Stressed? Frustrated? Out of control?

Let's look at the behaviour of people who live this way. Every day they are focusing on getting through the day and preparing for tomorrow. In other words they react and focus on the future. They use time to measure their lives, whether it's a minute, an hour, a day, a year or a lifetime. When they reach old age, what is their biggest regret? That they didn't spend more time with their children, partner, friends and so on – it's never not spending more time at work! They have forgotten to live in the moment and not be distracted by demands around them. When we live in the moment we stay focused on what is important.

Exercise

Answer these questions. They will help you gain control and learn to live in the moment.

What are my strengths?

What do I deeply enjoy doing?

What have been my happiest moments in life (work and non-work)?

Why were they happy?

When I look at my work life, what activities have the greatest worth?

What results am I getting?

What would produce better results?

What are the most important goals I want to fulfil?

The difficulties

The issue of time is a whole book in itself, but when connecting with people it is important to make the time to connect with the clarity of what you want from those connections to enhance your human capital.

The second barrier is the feeling that making connections is difficult because it isn't important in a world where you are judged by how well you do alone. In the western world in particular, the emphasis has been on 'the individual'. This has been reinforced with laws that protect the 'rights of the individual'. We regard ourselves as unique but also isolated. How often have you had a problem at work and felt there was no one to talk it over with? This isolation affects both our personal and working lives and is made worse by the strong belief throughout organizations that work is not the place for emotions.

We regard ourselves as unique but also isolated

When I worked in a large corporate during the 1980s it was frowned upon to have 'friends' at work; instead the emphasis was on 'colleagues' who were just people you happened to work with. Yet when I had worked for a newspaper where every day the pressure of deadlines was immense, relief often came at some point during the day with a 'moment of madness' a few minutes of fun and laughter. Over time real friendships formed and this generated a good feeling of teamwork. However, the most noticeable difference was the energy levels. In the corporate world you did your work as best you could, but at the newspaper some days we would literally 'buzz' with energy and would work flat out to achieve more than expected.

The whole physical universe is energy, including human beings, as we too are made from atoms. The trees, the rocks, animals and people, the products that we make all share the basic ingredient of energy. When we realize this, it becomes clear that we are all connected in a field of energy, to others and to all life. Therefore making connections is a natural process.

When we stop treating networking as selling and see it as connecting, informing, learning, supporting or being part of something exciting, we enter a network with a different stance and you will find people will come to you. Social capital is about connecting and building relationships. This sounds straightforward, but like many things is in fact far from it. Building relationships has something very important at its core – trust. So we need to look at how you build relationships as part of your human capital.

Exercise

Make a list of the people you work with and identify those you trust, or customers you trust. When you have done this, note down why you trust them.

Trust forms over time when people behave consistently. This means that they do what they say they will do and treat everyone fairly. You can always expect honesty and openness from people you trust, even if it means telling you something difficult. How can you capture this in connecting with others in a network? The best way is to open the channels of communication and use something called 'dialogue'.

Connecting through dialogue

We often use the word dialogue to mean conversation, but dialogue is much more than talking. Dialogue originated in Ancient Greece where the philosopher Socrates used it to teach his students. The Greek translation of dialogue is 'through relationship'. Socrates used dialogue as a form of ongoing conversation with his students whereby he would ask them specific questions that challenged their thinking, beliefs, assumptions and so on. His aim was to get to the truth that he regarded as deep within us. This links with Chapter 5.

Dialogue explores our closely held values

Therefore dialogue explores our closely held values, our mental models and inherited cultural beliefs. When we use dialogue to connect with others we explore deeply the individuals, their values, motivations, beliefs, assumptions, so that very quickly the group can learn from the different experiences of those involved, really get to know each other and build trust and develop new understandings. In this way the emphasis for the network is on information and learning rather than selling.

In more modern times, dialogue was developed and practised by physicist and philosopher David Bohm. He believed that people have an innate capacity for collective intelligence and as we explored in the chapter on intellectual capital, people possess significant tacit knowledge deep inside. Bohm believed that this knowledge and information could be unblocked through dialogue. In a network where people come together because of a common interest or purpose, the environment is conducive to developing dialogue to strengthen the connections and learn. This does not mean that those involved will always agree. In fact, at times the process will be frustrating and difficult, but when the agreed outcome is shared learning, it is worth the commitment.

Dialogue focuses on questions, listening, exploration, sharing, learning and respect. Making connections through networking now takes a larger context. The group become close and the emphasis is on learning. Finally, the connections are based on an equal footing of giving and taking knowledge from the group. Once this connection is strong the network can explore work issues in a larger context and decide actions they can take, thus enabling the network to also have an outcome. The key difference with this form of networking is the strength of the relationships that evolve.

chapter eight
building relationships

Participation and relationships are that part of your human capital where you express who you are in the world. We cannot influence any situation without respect for the complex network of people in an organization and those outside it such as customers.

To build relationships you need to establish trust and the only way to do this is to be authentic, open, honest and consistent. What does this mean? Being authentic means knowing who you really are and expressing that. Being consistent requires us to do what we say.

Each day many people put on a 'uniform' and go to work where they behave in what their culture considers to be the accepted way. An insurance company, for example, may expect employees to be 'big', brash, smartly dressed in suits, confident, male, slapping each other on the back and raving about beating off competitors. Many people go to work and play a role to comply with the accepted norm but they feel the strain of this after a time. Therefore being authentic is not easy for many people.

Being authentic is not easy for many people

You can walk into organizations today in both the public and private sectors and meet sceptical employees who go to work, do a job, giving no more or less than what is required to survive, and go home where their lives become interesting. Why has this happened?

Time and time again these people have seen directors and managers say one thing and express another in their actions and behaviour. A typical example is when a director says: 'We really care about our people and want a diverse workforce of intelligent workers.' But then the workers see colleagues being dismissed, especially those who don't 'fit in'. Sometimes employees see their seniors rewarded for incompetence while performance is appraised for them with targets that seem unreachable.

Building trust at work is impossible in this kind of environment. However, the challenge for you is to make authenticity and consistency part of your development plan towards growing your human capital. Chapter 3, on self-knowledge, will help. When you express your authentic self, building relationships through networks will be positive. But the challenge doesn't end here. Building relationships requires even more work.

How successful you are at building relationships will also depend on three other relationships: the relationship you have with yourself, how you see others, and accepting how others see you.

Three relationships

The quality of the relationship you have with yourself determines the quality of all other relationships because life reflects back to you who you think you are.

Exercise

Tackle these questions with honesty and give answers that are more than 'yes' or 'no'.

Do you like yourself?

What do you like/dislike?

Do you think you are a worthy human being?

Why?

Do you trust yourself?

Why?

Do you deserve happiness/success and so on?

Why?

Where did the beliefs that these answers are based on come from?

The answers will be reflected in the relationships you have with others.

When we looked at world knowledge it showed that different people have different 'realities' and as such we should respect those differences and view them as opportunities to develop our own understanding of life. We tend to choose friends who have similar realities and worldviews to our own – in other words we seek assurance. In networking we will meet individuals who differ in their beliefs and worldviews and this should be perceived as healthy rather than a matter of conflict. In this situation your authenticity is vital as well as how you feel about yourself. If the relationship with yourself is negative, different worldviews can seem threatening. Therefore relationships with others will be limited.

Finally, no matter how good or clever you are you will need other people to help you reach your goals and these people will sometimes view you in a different way to how you view yourself. Occasionally, one of these people may appear difficult, but it is important to remember that the difficult relationships are there for us to learn something about ourselves, reveal our deficiencies or deal with something that needs our attention. Therefore the information you find when developing relationships is not always technical or related to your work – it is related to you.

This brings us on to the openness you need. We need to be open to experiences and the opportunities that come from networking. We need to be open to all opportunities to network with the aim of gaining information, support and learning. The first step in building relationships is to listen and ask the other person what they do. Here the interest you show must be genuine. Then tell people what you do and it's amazing how many of them will say: 'You ought to talk to …' So the people you meet will be a catalyst to put you in touch with others.

Whenever you meet new people, always begin by asking about them. When you show an interest in another person they are more likely to listen to you and share information with you. Be open, honest and authentic for then what people see is the real you and this is what they seek. Remember, the Persona is not you.

Be open, honest and authentic

Don't feel awkward about asking for help or information. When we ask for help we are in reality giving another human being the opportunity to show their authenticity and greatness of spirit. It should be perceived to be an honour to ask for help or information.

Building relationships is part of developing your human capital and will become more relevant in the next couple of years as interconnections become the reality in everything we do. Why is it necessary to build relationships apart from the ability to network? The answer is to influence what happens around you. Therefore we need to understand what influencing really is and how to do it.

Influence

The first thing is to understand the difference between power and influence as we have the potential for both. Influence is an active process whereby one person or group modifies the attitudes or behavior of another person or group. Therefore, influence has been successful only when there is a change in attitudes, beliefs or behavior. For example, a decision is made to have a coffee vending machine put into the office. Most of the employees prefer to drink water, so they influence the decision maker to have a water dispenser put in as well.

Power, on the other hand, is a resource that gives a person or group the potential to influence another person or group. In other words, possession of power does not in itself enable a person to bring about change in the behaviour of others. Only if power is utilized in an effective way can one person influence another.

Individuals in any role in any organization have some power

Individuals in any role in any organization have some power, some potential or ability to influence others. The amount of power that one person has in relation to another depends upon the other person's perception of that power, how strong they believe it to be, whether the other particular power base has any value or meaning for them, and whether they believe that the power will actually be used in an attempt to influence them.

To influence someone you need the other person to listen to you with an open mind and then to respond. But to do this they have to trust you and see you as a credible person. We have explored trust but not credibility. Credibility is based on what you project as well as how you behave. If you feel you are not credible, then you will not project that. If you behave without credibility you will not have the respect of others. Once you have trust and credibility you can influence.

chapter nine
recognizing synchronicity

Have you ever noticed that sometimes things come together without effort in an almost unbelievable way? A colleague suggested I meet someone in California who had written books on a subject I was interested in. Two days later I saw this author on television speaking about her work. The next day I was invited to the wedding of a dear friend in California so I am now flying out to attend the wedding and meet the author.

Sometimes events in our lives lead us to feel we are being guided down a path we are meant to follow.

Exercise

Think of a situation when everything just flowed and happened with ease. It could be outside of work, it doesn't matter, the important thing is to acknowledge an example of this phenomenon. How did it feel? Use words to describe it.

This process was first described by Carl Jung in 'Synchronicity: An Acausal Connecting Principle' (*The Structure and Dynamics of the Psyche*, Princeton University Press, 1960). Here he defined synchronicity as 'a meaningful coincidence of two or more events, where something other than the probability of chance is involved'. It is as if forces outside our control make things come together or happen.

This phenomenon was recognized thousands of years ago in Taoism and it was eastern knowledge and understanding that influenced Jung and Richard Wilhelm, with whom he worked on developing this concept. Jung's studies led him to believe that our everyday understanding of the nature of time and space was limited. His ideas about synchronicity then developed from meetings with the well-known quantum physicists Einstein and Heisenberg. What evolved from these meetings was the recognition that time does not go forward in a straight line. Time, space and events coexist in a way that is beyond the normal understanding of our five senses. But what if we evolve beyond these senses?

Author Gary Zukov believes this is happening to more and more people. He explains that the world we see is a physical one and that our present senses enable us to deal with this physical world. However, what he calls 'multisensory' humans extend beyond a physical reality to an invisible realm. They recognize their inner wisdom and spirit or soul and differentiate this from their personality. He argues that although a personality can be compassionate, love, wisdom and compassion come from the soul rather than the personality.

Trusting the universe

To develop our human capital, we must trust ourselves and the universe. When we trust the universe, we allow synchronicity to enter our lives.

When synchronicity happens, go with it

When synchronicity happens, go with it. Don't stop and analyze. Yes, be alert and aware, but accept that what is happening is natural. My experience is that synchronicity often occurs as part of connecting with others and as such is part of social capital. Another aspect of synchronicity and the universe is that it doesn't always occur when you want it to. There seems to be a 'right time' outside our control – a time for the universe that is different from our own. The key is to stop trying to control and instead let go and trust the universe. What does it feel like? Go back to your experience of synchronicity and remember the feeling. When synchronicity is around, there is a feeling of 'flow'.

American psychologist Mihaly Csikszentmihalyi studied for many years what he calls 'flow experiences'. These are times of effortless action which people have described as feeling like ecstasy, 'being in the zone' and 'when time stands still'. A composer described the experience to Csikszentmihalyi as: 'You yourself are in an ecstatic state to such a point that you feel as though you almost don't exist. I've experienced this time and again. My hand seems devoid of myself, and I have nothing to do with what is happening. I just sit there watching in a state of awe and wonderment. And it just flows out by itself' (Daniel Goleman, *Emotional Intelligance*, Bantam, 1995).

In flow

You know you have had flow experiences when you become lost in an activity that requires concentration and challenges your existing skills. Csikszentmihalyi found, after two decades of study, that what marks these moments as different from others is that they usually involve clear goals. However, not all goals result in flow. The feelings associated with flow are joy and rapture and are therefore rewarding in themselves.

My experience of this phenomenon can be explained with two examples. The first was the work I accomplished with the RAF's Red Arrows that culminated in my book *Creating Top Flight Teams* (Kogan Page, 1996). The work 'flowed' and the experience was exciting and joyous because I knew I was discovering something new and important about how high-performing teams work. It led me to work in countries I had never thought I would see, and helping teams succeed on a global basis was incredibly rewarding. This all came from little 'effort' but a great deal of everything just 'happening'.

The second example was more recent. A colleague rang me one Sunday morning with an idea for a project. At first I was dubious but suddenly, talking to others, the project took on a momentum of its own. This momentum became global and people were drawn to us and the project from all around the world. Again, the feeling was one of 'happening' rather than 'effort'. It felt like 'an exciting place to be'.

Both these experiences had goals, but what made them different to other projects was that it seemed they were 'meant to happen'. That was just how it felt. From these experiences it is clear that synchronicity is a real phenomenon that we should tap into as part of developing our human capital.

Is it different to what Maslow called self-actualization? Both appear to involve this 'losing oneself in something'. In a state of flow, people become totally absorbed in what they are doing, merging their awareness with their actions and losing all self-consciousness, much like those in a state of self-actualization studied by Maslow.

Csikszentmihalyi offers ways to increase your flow experiences at work by suggesting they occur when you are emotionally involved in your job and anyone impacted by it. To achieve this I believe the work has to reflect your inner values. Flow experience can occur when we intentionally focus on a task close to our heart that will slightly stretch our skills. Csikszentmihalyi writes: 'People seem to concentrate best when the demands on them are a bit greater than usual, and they are able to give more than usual. If there is too little demand on them, people are bored. If there is too much for them to handle, they get anxious. Flow occurs in that delicate zone between boredom and anxiety' (*Emotional Intelligence*).

I believe the work has to reflect your inner values

Exercise

Answer this question:

What part of your work is important to you?

Put it into the context of goals with an outcome.

Now focus on how you will achieve this and spend 20 minutes brainstorming and planning using your creativity, knowledge, skills and intuition.

Meaning, not targets

In organizations today the motivators tend to be targets, threats, financial rewards and status. None of these will lead to flow. To develop whole people who can express their human capital requires another approach. People want meaning and purpose in their work – this is the motivator above all else. Csikszentmihalyi concludes: 'Painters must want to paint above all else. If the artist in front of the canvas begins to wonder how much he will sell it for, or what the critics will think of it, he won't be able to pursue original avenues. Creative achievements depend on single-minded immersion' (*Emotional Intelligence*).

Think of the last time you were totally immersed in something. It could have been listening to music or working on a project. In expressing human capital we need to have more of these flow experiences and they should begin in childhood.

Howard Gardner from Harvard University shared his views on flow in children's development with Daniel Goleman who recorded them.

'Flow is an internal state that signifies a kid is engaged in a task that's right. You have to find something you like and stick to it. It's when kids get bored in school that they fight and act up, and when they're overwhelmed by a challenge that they get anxious about their schoolwork. But you learn at your best when you

have something you care about and you can get pleasure from
being engaged in.'

(*Emotional Intelligence*)

It is the same for us in our working lives. However, I see a difference
between flow and synchronicity that is worth mentioning. Both
experiences are relevant and important to developing our human
capital. Flow seems to happen when a person is engrossed in an
activity and the emphasis comes from that person. From it we feel
the most incredible coming together of who we really are. When we
are in flow we are expressing who we are.

Synchronicity occurs when a project or task unfolds but the exiting
coincidences seem to come from *outside* the person. It is as if we give
out something from ourselves and the 'universe' responds. From it
we feel we are on our right path, our purpose of why we are here.
Again we experience joy but with the events that are occurring in our
world rather than with something from inside ourselves.

In developing our human capital we need to experience and learn
from both.

However, where synchronicity seems to have a special ability is that
it occurs collectively with people from different parts of the world. It
is as if events are meant to happen and when we make the right
choices, the universe opens a path for us. In developing our human
capital we should learn to trust this phenomenon and accept that we
live in a world of possibilities. Nothing ever happens by accident.
Everything that happens is meant for a reason that often we don't
recognize until much later. As humans we make mistakes, but when
we make the right choices, our intentions are heard and things
happen in a synchronous way.

It is as if events are meant to happen

Synchronicity is the antithesis of control or manipulation. We need to
accept that there is so much about our existence that we still do not
understand and may never fully understand. So we have to accept
and trust as part of being the best we can be.

04

part four
emotional capital

chapter ten
emotional intelligence

On the day after Christmas a man in Boston went to work and shot seven colleagues because he was so angry with them for saying they were going to direct some of his wages to pay outstanding tax. This true story is an example of how powerful our emotions can be.

Yet many people in cultures such as the English and Japanese learn that it is not 'good manners' to express too much emotion and keep it locked up inside. Is this right?

Our emotions are part of who we are and as such are part of our human capital. According to Daniel Goleman we all have two minds: one that thinks and one that feels. Through their interaction we construct our mental life. The way we live our lives is determined by both our intellectual and emotional intelligences. Most of the time in our day-to-day lives, the two are in balance, but when passions rise, the emotional will always have the upper hand. What emotional intelligence tries to do is to recognize the need to harmonize the two.

When passions rise, the emotional will always have the upper hand

The focus of academic learning has been on logical intelligence, to the neglect of the emotional mind, and yet we know that 'success' in life – in work, relationships and so on – is not based on logical intelligence but on emotional intelligence (EQ). Therefore EQ must be included in our human capital.

EQ writer Daniel Goleman defines emotional intelligence as 'the capacity for recognizing our own feelings and those of others, for motivating ourselves, and for managing emotions well in ourselves and in our relationships' (*Emotional Intelligence*).

If we want to develop our emotional intelligence as part of our human capital, where do we begin? There is a natural link here back to Chapter 3 – self-awareness, or rather being aware of your internal states. According to John Mayer of the University of New Hampshire, self-awareness involves being aware of our moods and thoughts about those moods. In fact, how are you feeling right now? Try this simple exercise to help you become aware of your emotions.

Answer these questions:

1. How do you behave when you feel upset?

2. Would other people describe you as an emotional person? What does that mean to you?

3. How do you respond when someone around you is critical or negative towards you?

4. Are you ever embarrassed by your own or others' emotions?

5. Is fear or anger a problem for you?

6. Do you wish you could feel happier, motivated or peaceful more often?

7. When you feel happy or loving can you hold on to those feelings?

8. How long do negative emotions last?

9. How long do positive emotions last?

10. Do you wait for positive feelings before doing whatever needs doing?

Different emotional styles

Mayer believes people have different emotional styles. The first are those who are aware of their moods as they are having them. They tend to have a positive outlook on life and when a bad mood takes over they don't spend time analyzing it but instead pull themselves out of it quickly.

The second style is recognized as those who feel swamped by their emotions and have difficulty escaping them. They don't feel any control over their emotional life and so accept and stay with their moods. At worst, they feel overwhelmed and out of control of their emotions.

The final style is one where people accept their feelings. Sometimes this can involve 'happy' individuals who are content to stay with their state. For others the mood is negative, but again they accept this. People who are depressed often stay with this mood rather than try to change it.

Which of these styles best describes you? Psychologist Suzanne Miller uses a scenario to identify the answer.

Exercise

Imagine you are on a plane flying from London to New York. Halfway across the Atlantic the captain speaks on the intercom: 'Ladies and Gentlemen, there's some turbulence ahead. Please return to your seats and fasten your seat belts.' In a few moments the plane hits the turbulence, which is far greater than you've ever experienced. The plane is tossed around like a beach ball on the waves. What do you do? Do you bury yourself in a book or magazine, or continue watching the movie? Do you take out the emergency card and read it or watch the flight attendants to see if they show signs of panic?

Those who would distract themselves notice less about their own reactions and so minimize the experience of their emotional response. Those who tune into their emotions end up amplifying the magnitude of their reactions and emotional awareness becomes overwhelming. What have you learned about yourself from this?

How can these emotions affect us at work? When emotions are overwhelming they can render us inactive. Our concentration and cognitive skills are affected and a simple task such as remembering a telephone number becomes impossible. Our emotions get in the way or enhance our capabilities to think and plan, to solve problems and make decisions every day.

In developing our human capital we need to be aware of this emotional part of who we are and address it with the aim of maintaining thinking and feeling in a healthy, balanced state. The heart of emotional intelligence is accepting your emotions and doing what you need to do despite what you are feeling.

Losing control

When we deny our feelings or ignore them, pressure builds and we are at risk of 'losing control'. We are denying our emotional authenticity. When we deny our emotions over time, we get physical symptoms, from headaches and backaches to hypertension and muscle stiffness. Ongoing restriction can create a condition called 'psychosclerosis' or hardening of the attitudes. People who 'harden' have a tendency to show this physically around the mouth as they grow older. In addition, physician Deepak Chopra believes that we carry our emotions around our body in our cells and if left they result in serious illnesses.

When we deny our emotions over time, we get physical symptoms

Exercise

How many emotions do we experience on a daily basis? On a fresh sheet of paper draw two vertical lines, making three columns. At the top of the page give each column a heading: Time, Activity, Feelings.

Every hour for one day fill in the columns. For example:

8.30am   Driving to work/driving child to school   Preoccupied/rushed

9.30am   Meeting with my boss   Don't feel appreciated

This will make you realize how important and varied our feelings are in a day. It really is worth doing this exercise for a day to see how your emotions change.

Next, an interesting way to discover more about your emotional intelligence. This is an exercise I first came across on a course and have since read in a couple of books.

Exercise

Imagine you are a four-year-old and you are offered the following choice. I'm in the room with you but I have to run an errand. If you wait until I get back, you can have two marshmallows. If you can't wait until then, you can have only one marshmallow but you can have it right now. Which do you choose? Make your choice now and write it down.

The choice tells us not only the character of the child but the trajectory that child is likely to take through life. This exercise was used at Stanford University during the 1960s with four-year-olds who were then studied until they graduated. The four-year-olds who waited did all sorts of things to minimize the temptation, such as covering their eyes so they couldn't see the marshmallows, playing games, talking to themselves or trying to sleep – anything to sustain their resolve for what seemed like a long time. Fifteen minutes later they received two marshmallows. For others, the temptation was too strong and they grabbed one marshmallow seconds after the experimenter had left the room, showing impulsive behaviour.

Twelve to fourteen years later, the difference between the two groups was apparent. Those who had resisted were more socially competent, personally effective, self-assertive and better able to cope with life. They thrived on challenges and pursued them even in adversity. These adolescents were confident, self-reliant, dependable, trustworthy, used initiative and were still able to delay reward in pursuit of their goals.

The few who had grabbed the one marshmallow were more likely to be shy, stubborn, indecisive, easily upset by difficulties, prone to jealousy, saw themselves as unworthy, were mistrustful and this led to fights as they felt they deserved their rewards now. Is our emotional intelligence mapped out by the age of four? Much of it is, but it doesn't mean we can't change it.

Healthy emotional intelligence means being positive

Healthy emotional intelligence means being positive and not giving up believing you have the will and the means to accomplish your goals. Being positive means seeing a failure as something that you can learn from and change so that success comes next time. The opposite and unhealthy emotion is to take responsibility for the failure, blaming it on a characteristic of yourself that cannot be changed.

Potential for learning

Our emotional intelligence determines our potential for learning. The areas we need to develop to improve emotional intelligence are:

◆ self-awareness, which is knowing what we are feeling and using this to guide our decisions. This includes being able to make a realistic assessment of our abilities and having a grounded sense of confidence;

- motivation, which uses our deepest preferences to move and guide us toward our goals, to help us take the initiative and to strive to improve our potential while persevering over setbacks;

- self-regulation, by handling our emotions so that they facilitate rather than block tasks, being able to delay reward to pursue goals and recover well from emotional distress;

- empathy, which involves sensing what others are feeling, understanding and accepting their perspective while building a rapport with a broad diversity of people;

- adeptness in relationships, by interacting well, using skills to influence, persuade, negotiate and settle disputes so that the aim is co-operation and teamwork.

There are further parts to your emotional capital that come not from emotional intelligence theories but from the ideas based on the work of psychologist Dr Eric Berne. Known as transactional analysis, or TA, this has developed since Berne's death in 1970 and is a huge subject. But what we are going to explore here is the difference between the authentic feelings you express and what I shall call 'learned' feelings.

As a child you will have learned that certain feelings were encouraged in your family while others were discouraged. When you experienced a discouraged feeling you will have switched quickly to an alternative accepted feeling. Therefore we grow up using learned feelings while we expressed authentic feelings before we learned to censor them. Does this matter? What has this got to do with your emotional capital as an adult?

Let's look at a couple of examples and follow them through to adulthood. A little girl learns that it is permitted to be sad in her family but not angry. As an adult she finds herself about to get angry because someone has pushed in front of her in the photocopier queue when she has a document to copy urgently. The moment she begins to feel angry she goes into her learned childhood pattern almost like a reflex. Instead of getting angry, she begins to feel sad and may be unable to stop bursting into tears. She has covered her authentic feeling of anger with the learned feeling of sadness. Colleagues will wonder why she is feeling sad but really she wants to express anger about the other person's rudeness.

Authentic emotions

The authentic emotions we tend to feel are anger, sadness, fear and gladness. When we express authentic emotions we can solve problems that we are unable to solve when we replace them with learned emotions. This is why understanding emotional capital is important to your human capital at work when you want to be your best. To show the 'power' of authentic feelings in problem solving, transactional analysis practitioner George Thomson found a time frame also came into play. He found that when we feel authentic *fear* and express it, we solve a problem that may arise in the *future*. For example, if you are crossing a road and a car appears from nowhere going very fast, the fear prompts you to act and leap to one side to avoid an impact. Therefore you avoid the future danger of being knocked down.

When we express authentic *anger* we solve problems in the *present*

When we express authentic *anger* we solve problems in the *present*. Let's go back to the photocopy machine. Someone pushes ahead of you, shoving you to one side. Expressing your anger you react to look after yourself in the present by pushing back and saying: 'I was here before you and also have an important document to copy. Please wait till I have finished.'

Finally, when you are feeling authentic *sadness* it is a natural process to overcome a painful event in the *past*. This is usually some kind of loss. By allowing yourself to be sad and cry you free yourself from that past pain and move forward into the present and future.

In contrast, the learned emotions do not have this problem-solving capability and therefore you need to be sure that the feelings you express are authentic. For example, being angry instead of sad will not help you with a past event. How do you know whether your feelings are authentic? At any time when you feel the emotions of sadness, anger or fear out of their correct time frame as shown here, the emotion is a learned feeling.

Emotional capital is a very important part of your human capital in developing the whole human being. In fact, Goleman says all emotions are impulses to act. This brings us on to the final part of your human capital – action.

the will to act

So now it's down to you! Dan Millman wrote:

'This world is a realm of energy and action; no matter what you know or who you are – no matter how many books you have read or what your talents – only action brings potential to life.'

(*No Ordinary Moments*, H.J. Kramer Inc, 1992)

Now we are close to the end of the book and the final section explores the will to act that is also part of your emotional capital. In the previous chapters you hopefully learned things about yourself as a full human being and the world we live in. However, this is futile if the commitment to do something with this new understanding is missing. And for this you will require two things: the *capability* and the *courage* to act.

So what stops us? Fear! The fear of change, the fear of making a fool of ourselves, the fear of mistakes, the fear of exposing our inner being, the fear of insecurity, and so on. So let's deal with this fear thing by simplifying it. Everything we do, every thought, every decision, every action, comes from one of two places: fear or love. If we don't trust others it is because of fear. When we fall deeply in love we very often face our fear at that moment – a fear that the other person won't love us in return or we will lose our love or the person will betray us.

If we don't trust others it is because of fear

Where do these fears come from? Most come from the past, and our parents often contribute to this. This does not mean we start blaming the past or our parents. Instead we acknowledge that an event in our past has led to our behaviour and fears in the present. In fact, we very often discover that a pattern of behaviour has been occurring for 10, 20, 30 years or more and that until we 'deal' with the past event our actions are limited or negative.

What a waste – to live a life of untapped potential because of fear. To reiterate what we have said before: the relationship you have with yourself affects all others. Yet fear is there to teach us. When we challenge fears, look them in the eye, they give us insights to help us grow, enabling us to move on. The problem is that we hide our fears; we dismiss them and pretend they don't exist. In this hidden place they loom big and frightening. Yet in the open light of day, when we look them in the eye and confront them, they are never as terrifying.

Operating from fear

At work we can either operate from fear to let the system or boss run us, or act to operate using our full human capital and enable the system to work for everyone and forever change the relationship with our boss. The will to act means influencing the world around us for the better and we do this by using our full human capital. John Gardner, professor of educational leadership at Seattle University, wrote: 'Our state of being is the real source of our ability to influence the world' (*Insights on Leadership*, edited by Larry C. Spears, John Wiley & Sons).

However, the hidden part of the iceberg that is not seen or used in work is often where your courage lies. It is sometimes easier to leave courage at home and justify this by telling ourselves that courage will speak and ruin our chances of promotion. So in the end we remain silent. An example of this was an individual who sat for five hours in a meeting that was totally unproductive and in which the majority were not even participating. He wanted to say: 'I've had enough of this. There must be a better way.' But he could not find the courage to speak out. Instead he left the meeting frustrated and exhausted – as did most of the others.

The bottom line is that we have a choice

The bottom line is that we have a choice: to ignore our fears and hope they will go away, or to look for the learning within our fears and derive positive benefits from them. The will to act requires the courage to make this choice. Kay Gilley says: 'Courage isn't courage if we don't continue to look fear in the face, to accept that fear is with us, and to move forward' (*Leading From the Heart*, Butterworth Heinemann, 1997).

Courage

The will to act means acting out of courage, intention and commitment. It requires as much courage to express our true feelings, break a habit or take the risk to be different and follow our heart as it requires to tackle a bank robber or save a child from drowning. We have to accept our humanity, accept that we only grow from our own efforts, while accepting that although action may be difficult or uncomfortable, we still do it.

You are now aware of your human capital. What is stopping you from using it? This is going to be a hard exercise but it will give you the greatest feeling of peace as you rid yourself of the fear.

Exercise

Write down who or what is stopping you from being the best you can be. Make a list of your fears.

Next to each item on your list try to identify the *real* cause of each. Look back in your past to answer this. Remember how you felt and write this down.

Really feel the pain and anguish you experienced and don't shut it off. You are not alone. Now go back to that moment and the people with you. Tell them how you feel and *forgive* them. This is not easy and don't worry if you feel emotional. These emotions need to be expressed. The forgiveness must come from your heart. To make it easier, say: 'I know you did/said what you said because you knew no better at the time.'

Now forgive you, the child or teenager, who was hurt and repeat: 'You reacted as you did because you knew no better.' Feel love for this younger you and realize that she/he deserves all your love. Feel the inner peace that comes from this. Now write down the actions you will take without the fear to stop you.

I know that exercise is hard because I've done it myself a few times. But you have so much potential inside you – don't allow the past to stop you becoming the best you can be. Learn from it and let it go. You will then find the courage to act.

Commitment

The will to act also requires commitment. This commitment is to your purpose – the problem is, most people do not know what their purpose is. Our purpose is not to make lots of money or aim to get a knighthood; we become our purpose when we make choices to be who we really are. Who are you? It is who you really want to be. Inside you really do have the answers. Margaret Lulic writes: 'There is greatness buried in every soul from the moment of birth ... to know we make a difference to someone or something beyond ourselves and even beyond our family' (*Who We Could Be at Work*, Butterworth Heinemann, 1996).

Having explored your human capital you need to ask: what do I really care about? What do I feel passionate about? What does my heart tell me it wants to do? Even if your answers seem unrealistic, write them down.

What do I feel passionate about?

If this is too difficult, go for a walk, listen to some music, sit on a beach – be with yourself for an hour and then answer the questions, for the answers truly are inside you – you won't find them on a course or from someone else, only from within yourself.

There are always excuses not to act, but instead ask: who will help me achieve my purpose? Recognize the difference between a job and a purpose. The Dalai Lama said: 'If you seek enlightenment for yourself simply to enhance yourself and your position, you miss your purpose; if you seek enlightenment for yourself to enable you to serve others, you are with purpose' (*Ancient Wisdom, Modern World*, Little Brown & Co, 1999).

When you have purpose you have direction to act out your human capital. This purpose is often an idea or a path, which entails periods of no view of where it will take you. This is where 'will' enters the frame. The will to act is about desire. You need to desire what you want and believe you deserve it. Yet there is an even greater will – this involves trusting the universe and your place in it to become all you are capable of. Writer and thinker Martin Buber describes something he calls the 'grand will': 'The free man is he who wills without arbitrary self-will' (*I and Thou*, Charles Schribner's Sons, 1970).

By this he means making a personal choice or chance instead of using reason. Buber goes on to explain that when 'grand will' comes into play, man (or woman) perceives a universe that is waiting for his/her action. Buber writes:

'He believes in destiny, and believes that it stands in need of him. It does not keep him in leading-strings, it awaits him, he must go to it, yet does not know where it is to be found. But he knows that he must go out with his whole being. The matter will not turn out according to his decision; but what is to come will come only when he decides on what he is able to will. He must sacrifice his puny, unfree will, that is controlled by things and instincts, to his grand will, which quits defined for destined being. Then he intervenes no more, but at the same time he does not let things merely happen. He listens to what is emerging from himself, to the course of being in the world; not in order to be supported by it, but in order to bring it to reality as it desires.'

(I and Thou)

The will to act is the last part of developing your human capital and it is the most difficult. It requires courage, purpose and trust along with your emotional capital. Fear is the enemy within and your emotional behaviour will be paramount in your actions. That does not mean that we should expect to live a life free of fear and difficulties. A Zen teacher said: 'Having many difficulties perfects the will; having no difficulties ruins the being.' The will to act is connected to the rest of your human capital. To develop your will you must take the first steps towards your purpose.

Exercise

Look at what you wrote down for what your heart longs to do. The last step in this section is to set down the first steps to take you there. List three actions to move you to your purpose. Put a date for when you are going to take each step and tick them as you take them. As you achieve one, add another step. Do this for six months and see what you achieve. The will to act must come from you and you alone – you cannot ask others for what you are not willing to do yourself.

05

part five
to be the best you can be

chapter twelve
fusing your human capital

Human capital is much more than knowledge and skills. Inside every employee is a complex, unique capital that has huge potential for the organization. However, much lies dormant for two reasons. The first is that the individual is not aware of their potential. The second is an outdated view of employees as a resource, much like equipment. Both these perceptions have resulted in limited success for individuals and organizations. This has to change in the 21st century. Individuals want to be the best they can be and express it at work where they spend so much time. The action and energy required for this is called fusion.

Every aspect of your human capital is linked and connected to enable you to be the best you can be. To begin developing your human capital you need to acknowledge that you have this ability within you. Working through the book you will have discovered things about yourself you were not aware of, as well as things you knew. You can see now that going on a training course will have limited results because you have the ability, potential and greatness already within you. The key is to take some time and seek what is there. Most training and development focuses on part of who you are. Here the focus has been on the whole human being.

Fusion

The final stage is to bring this together – to fuse your human capital. To fuse is to join or combine. Fusion in the field of physics is about coming together and creating connections. Instead of splitting the atom, fusion joins together atomic nuclei and produces five times the energy of splitting the atom. When fusing your whole human capital the same effect will occur.

Fusion is also about seeing similarities rather than differences

Fusion is also about seeing similarities rather than differences. To explain your human capital we took the elements apart, but in doing so we omit the similarities between the parts and instead focus on the differences in each element. We now have to fuse your human capital to see the connections. You will then see overlap, similarities and relationships between the elements making up your human capital (see Figure 12.1).

Figure 12.1 Your human capital

We have to connect all the aspects that make up the unique human being. In the diagram you can see all the elements that are connected to each other. What a diagram won't show is that the elements are not static. They move around, grow and change shape, enabling the host body to change from deep inside. Growing your human capital is not about physical growth – it is about personal growth within you.

Knowledge capital we saw was more than analytical data; it included explicit and tacit knowledge. This includes the facts and information your brain stores and your personal experience. This is the unique knowledge you bring to work that is hard to capture in a workplace that doesn't allow people to experiment and explore their tacit knowledge.

Self-knowledge affects how we express ourselves in the world and how we conduct relationships with those around us. It includes our beliefs, values, self-esteem, masculine and feminine attributes, our introvert/extrovert preference and ego. Understanding this part of our human capital is an ongoing process as we change through new experiences and learning. Self-knowledge affects every other part of our human capital.

Creative knowledge is not a gift for the few but the potential of all. It is encouraged in childhood but blocked in adult life. Therefore to rediscover creativity we can use playing to break through the blocks. Inner wisdom includes intuition and right-brain activity but also the unconscious mind. The key to unlocking inner wisdom is to be silent to enable us to hear it.

World knowledge is not the information we hear on the news but an evolving understanding of our universe. The greater this knowledge, the more we understand life and so are effective in the world. Recent understanding shows a shift from a machine-like understanding of the world, where control was the order for people, to a world of connections, relationships and the need for adaptability.

This links to social knowledge, where the focus is on networks and relationships to build common ground and knowledge (linking to the first aspect of human capital we explored). When we connect we can influence the world around us. However, we also need to understand and trust the world for it produces phenomena such as synchronicity. When we are focused on our work we experience flow and together work and life unfold. Trusting the world is important, but this does not mean we sit back and wait – the last part of human capital we explored was the will to act, where courage and purpose have an important contribution.

For Jung the most important goal for individuals was what he called 'individuation' – the process by which we become truly ourselves, the complete human beings we were born to be. He believed every life had a unique journey towards this. The process involved stripping away our masks and pretences and finding our true vocation.

Individuation

The process of becoming more complete reveals how the universal human traits and possibilities are combined in each individual in a unique way. At the same time, we discover that we share universal psychological patterns and energy systems which are present in the subconsciousness of each person yet are made up in infinite combinations to create individual psyches. We each have our own values, our own ways of life that make us much more than a clique of people. We must focus on recognizing and valuing the whole individual that is more than the Persona, the image we show to the world.

We each have our own values

This thinking fits in very much with the notion of developing our human capital – evolving to develop the whole human being to be the best they can be doing work that has meaning and purpose. In fact, Jung believed that our search for meaning is the most powerful motivating force. Viktor Frankl agreed with this. Using his experience of captivity in a Nazi camp for Jews to understand why some people survived while others lost hope and perished, he developed the theory that striving to find meaning in one's life is our primary motivational force. He believed that this meaning is unique and specific to an individual and as such, the meaning can be fulfilled only by that individual. When this occurs Frankl says it will satisfy that individual's *will* to meaning.

How strong is the need for meaning in your life? Do you have it from your work? How do you get meaning in your life? One way is to let your core values drive you rather than incentives such as a certain size salary. This way you are following your true authentic self and that will take you to finding your meaning or purpose.

The nearest description of this must be the feeling of what Abraham Maslow describes as self-actualization. He writes: 'Self-actualizing people are, without one single exception, involved in a cause outside their own skin, in something outside of themselves. They are devoted, working at something, something that is very precious to them' (*The Farther Reaches of Human Nature*).

Self-actualization

Maslow went on to describe the process of self-actualization as eight steps. The first requires the individual to experience fully, selflessly, with full concentration and absorption. This is what he says is the self-actualizing moment – to be fully immersed in what one is doing.

Secondly, the choices we make every day should be progression rather than regression choices. Maslow defined regression as when we allow ourselves to make defensive or risk-averse choices rather than growth choices. He says the former are based on being afraid. Growth choices are about being honest. Do I stay in a job I hate with a boss who is getting me down?

The third point is that we have a self to be actualized and we should let this self emerge. It requires listening to our self instead of to parents and colleagues. Allowing self to emerge can mean changing negative beliefs about ourselves. The fourth point is to trust our inner judgement and in doing so, by looking within ourselves for answers, we are taking responsibility. That in itself is a step towards self-actualization.

The fifth point is that we should recognize when we 'know' our destiny – what we are here for. People ask me how you know and all I can say is that when you are doing what you were meant to do it requires less effort. The path is less strewn with large boulders and people enter your life to help. The sixth step is to realize that self-actualization is not an end state but a process of actualizing one's potentialities. In other words, self-actualization is a journey without knowing the destination.

Self-actualization is a journey without knowing the destination

The seventh point is to experience 'peak experiences'. Here Maslow struggled and was never able to fully explain this, but he said it was the moment of ecstasy we feel when something flows. In this state, he said, his subjects said the world was more beautiful, more honest, more true. We have already explored the notion of flow and should now recognize it as we develop our human capital.

Finally, Maslow's eighth step involves finding out who we are. This means identifying our defences and finding the courage to give them up, which is often unpleasant and difficult. Here he argues: 'Implicit is a belief that truth heals much. Learning to break through one's repressions, to know one's self, to hear the impulse voices, to uncover the triumphant nature, to reach knowledge, insight and the truth – these are the requirements.'

The French writer Simone de Beauvoir said: 'I tore myself away from the safe comfort of certainties through my love for truth; and truth rewarded me.'

What is your truth?

'The more you are, the more you can become, and the more you can become, the more you can yet be. The deepest secret is that life is not a process of discovery, but a process of creation. You are not discovering yourself, but creating yourself anew. Seek, therefore, not to find out Who You Are, seek to determine Who You Want to Be.'

(Neale Donald Walsch, *Conversations With God, Book One*, Putnam, 1996)

This is the goal of developing your human capital. The potential to be great is there. Now you have discovered more about who you are, the final question is: who do you want to be? Write down the answer to this question, then focus on becoming this every day by making the right choices that will create the self you want to be. When you develop all your human capital you take a path that will ultimately lead you to your life's work. Good luck.

appendix

Learning styles questionnaire

This questionnaire and analysis was developed by HR specialists Honey and Mumford in the 1980s as a way to discover your preference for learning. It will explain why some learning is easier than others. Part of developing your human capital should include developing the ways of learning you find more difficult.

There are no right or wrong answers and it is best to answer as fast as you can with honesty rather than what you think the answer should be. If you agree more than disagree with each statement, put a tick next to it. If you disagree more than agree, put a cross. Make sure you put a tick or cross next to *every* statement.

1. I have strong beliefs about what is right and wrong, good and bad.

2. I often act without considering the possible consequences.

3. I tend to solve problems using a step-by-step approach.

4. I believe that formal procedures and policies restrict people.

5. I have a reputation for saying what I think, simply and directly.

6. I often find that actions based on feelings are as sound as those based on careful thought and analysis.

7. I like the sort of work where I have time for thorough preparation and implementation.

8. I regularly question people about their basic assumptions.

9. What matters most is whether something works in practice.

10. I actually seek out new experiences.

11. When I hear about a new approach or idea I immediately start working out how to apply it in practice.

12. I am keen on self-discipline, such as watching my diet, taking regular exercise, sticking to a fixed routine, etc.

13. I take pride in doing a thorough job.

14. I get on best with logical, analytical people and less well with spontaneous, 'irrational' people.

15. I take over the interpretation of data available to me and avoid jumping to conclusions.

16. I like to reach a decision carefully after weighing up my alternatives.

17. I am attracted more to novel, unusual ideas than to practical ones.

18. I don't like disorganization and prefer to fit things into a coherent pattern.

19. I accept and stick to laid-down procedures and policies as long as I regard them as an efficient way of getting the job done.

20. I like to relate my actions to a general principle.

21. In discussions I like to get straight to the point.

22. I have to have distant, rather formal relationships with people at work.

23. I thrive on the challenge of tackling something new and different.

24. I enjoy fun-loving, spontaneous people.

25. I pay meticulous attention to detail before coming to a conclusion.

26. I find it difficult to produce ideas on impulse.

27. I believe in coming to the point immediately.

28. I am careful not to jump to conclusions too quickly.

29. I prefer to have as many sources of information as possible – the more data to think over the better.

30. Flippant people who don't take things seriously enough usually irritate me.

31. I listen to other people's points of view before putting my own forward.

32. I tend to be open about how I'm feeling.

33. In discussions I enjoy watching the manoeuvring of other participants.

34. I prefer to respond to events on a spontaneous, flexible basis rather than plan things out in advance.

35. I tend to be attracted to techniques such as network analysis, flow charts, branching programmes, contingency planning, etc.

36. It worries me if I have to rush out a piece of work to meet a tight deadline.

37. I tend to judge people's ideas on their practical merits.

38. Quiet, thoughtful people make me uneasy.

39. I often get irritated by people who want to rush things.

40. It is more important to enjoy the present moment than to think about the past or future.

41. I think that decisions based on a thorough analysis of all the information are sounder than those based on intuition.

42. I tend to be a perfectionist.

43. In discussions, I usually produce lots of spontaneous ideas.

44. In meetings I put forward practical, realistic ideas.

45. More often than not, rules are there to be broken.

46. I prefer to stand back from a situation and consider all the perspectives.

47. I can often see inconsistencies and weaknesses in other people's arguments.

48. On balance I talk more than I listen.

49. I can often see better, more practical ways to get things done.

50. I think written reports should be short and to the point.

51. I believe that rational, logical thinking should win the day.

52. I tend to discuss specific things with people rather than engaging in social discussion.

53. I like people who approach things realistically rather than theoretically.

54. In discussions, I get impatient with irrelevancies and digressions.

55. If I have a report to write I produce lots of drafts before settling on the final version.

56. I am keen to try things out to see if they work in practice.

57. I am keen to reach answers via a logical approach.

58. I enjoy being the one who talks a lot.

59. In discussions I often find I am a realist, keeping people to the point and avoiding wild speculations.

60. I like to ponder many alternatives before making up my mind.

61. In discussions with people I often find I am the most dispassionate and objective.

62. In discussions I am more likely to adopt a 'low profile' than to take the lead and do most of the talking.

63. I like to be able to relate current actions to a longer-term bigger picture.

64. When things go wrong I am happy to shrug them off and put it down to experience.

65. I tend to reject wild, spontaneous ideas as being impractical.

66. It's best to think carefully before taking action.

67. On balance I do the listening rather than the talking.

68. I tend to be tough on people who find it difficult to adopt a logical approach.

69. Most times I believe the ends justify the means.

70. I don't mind hurting other people's feelings so long as the job gets done.

71. I find the formality of having specific objectives and plans stifling.

72. I'm usually one of the people who puts life into a party.

73. I do whatever is expedient to get the job done.

74. I quickly get bored with methodical, detailed work.

75. I am keen on exploring the basic assumptions, principles and theories underpinning things and events.

76. I'm always interested to find out what people think.

77. I like meetings to be run on methodical lines, sticking to a laid-down agenda, etc.

78. I steer clear of subjective or ambiguous topics.

79. I enjoy the drama and excitement of a crisis situation.

80. People often find me insensitive to their feelings.

Honey & Mumford, 1986

Please turn over for scoring.

Scoring

Score one point for each statement marked with a tick. No points are
scored for those with a cross.

2	7	1	5
4	13	3	9
6	15	8	11
10	16	12	19
17	25	14	21
23	28	18	27
24	29	20	35
32	31	22	37
34	33	26	44
38	36	30	49
40	39	42	50
43	41	47	53
45	46	51	54
48	52	57	56
58	55	61	59
64	60	63	65
71	62	68	69
72	66	75	70
74	67	77	73
79	76	78	80
Activist	Reflector	Theorist	Pragmatist

Learning descriptions

Activists

Activists involve themselves fully in new experiences. They enjoy the here and now and are happy to be dominated by immediate experiences. They are open minded and enthusiastic about anything new. They revel in short-term 'crisis' and tackle problems by brainstorming. They thrive on challenges but are bored with implementation and long-term consolidation. They are gregarious and tend to seek all activities around themselves.

Reflectors

Reflectors like to stand back and ponder experiences. They collect data and chew things over before coming to any conclusion. They tend to be cautious and thoughtful. They enjoy taking a back seat and observing people listening before making their own points. They often have an unruffled, easy air about them. When they act it is as part of a wide picture that includes the past as well as the present and others' observations as well as their own.

Theorists

Theorists adapt and integrate observations into complex but logical theories. They think problems through in a step-by-step way. They tend to be perfectionists who like things to fit into a rational scheme. They are keen on theories, models and principles and tend to be detached and analytical rather than subjective. They rigidly reject anything that does not fit with this mindset.

Pragmatists

Pragmatists are keen on trying new ideas, theories and techniques to see if they work in practice and take the first opportunity to experiment. They like to get on with things and act quickly and confidently on ideas that attract them. They hate 'beating around the bush' and can be impatient with ruminating. They want to see things happen in reality.

appendix

grow your personal capital

momentum

Learning for you

If your preferred style is the *activist*, you will learn best from activities that involve:

◆ new experiences or opportunities;

◆ high visibility;

◆ the generation of ideas with no constraints or structure;

◆ you being thrown in at the deep end;

◆ interactivity with others to bounce ideas off and solve problems.

If your preferred style is the *reflector*, you will learn best from activities that involve:

◆ watching or standing back;

◆ allowing you to think before doing;

◆ carrying out research or investigation;

◆ the opportunity to review what happened;

◆ time to reach a decision without tight deadlines.

If your preferred style is the *theorist*, you will learn best from situations that involve:

◆ time to methodically explore interrelationships between ideas and situations;

◆ the chance to question and probe the methodology or assumptions behind something;

◆ you being intellectually stretched or by teaching high calibre people who ask searching questions;

◆ listening to or reading ideas and concepts that emphasize logic or rationality and that are well argued;

◆ structured situations with a clear purpose.

If your preferred style is the *pragmatist,* you will learn best from activities where:

◆ there is an obvious link between the subject and a problem or opportunity and your job;

◆ you have the chance to try out and practice techniques with coaching/feedback from a credible expert;

◆ you are exposed to a model you can emulate, such as someone with a proven record, a respected boss or a film showing how it's done;

◆ you are given immediate opportunities to implement what you have learned;

◆ you can concentrate on practical issues.

recommended reading

This is just a handful of recommended books to continue the journey of developing your human capital. But remember, you can find learning in everything around you – people, films, books and events. The key is to see learning as a way of life.

Frankl, Viktor E., 1984, *Man's Search for Meaning*, Simon & Schuster Inc.

Goleman, Daniel, 1998, *Working with Emotional Intelligence*, Bantam.

Jaworski, Joseph, 1996, *Synchronicity – The Inner Path of Leadership*, Berrett-Koehler Inc.

Jeffers, Susan, 1996, *End the Struggle and Dance with Life*, DIANE Publishing.

Knighht, Sue, 1995, *NLP at Work*, Nicholas Brealey Ltd.

Maslow, A.H., 1976, *The Farther Reaches of Human Nature*, Penguin Books.

Nelson Bolles, Richard, 2000, *What Color is My Parachute*, Ten Speed Press.

Owen, Hilarie, 2000, *In Search of Leaders*, John Wiley & Sons.

Senge, Peter, 1990, *The Fifth Discipline*, Currency/Doubleday.

Simpson, Liz, 1999, *Working from the Heart*, Random House.

CPSIA information can be obtained at www.ICGtesting.com
Printed in the USA
BVOW08s1417131213

338979BV00002B/7/A